Fixing American Government

Ending Gridlock And Apathy With a 21st Century Constitution

By Jeffrey R. Orenstein, Ph.D.

First Edition: January 2015

Printed in the United States of America

Suncoast Digital Press, Inc.

ISBN: 978-1-93923732-3

Contents

Preface iii

PART I: **Democracy 1**

Chapter One: Democracy: An Enduring Political Ideal and Practice . . .3

Chapter Two: Democracy In America:
Alexis de Tocqueville's Vision and Influence. 9

Chapter Three: Democracy, Republic or Hybrid:
The Founders' Republicanism 13

PART II: **21st Century Problems and Prospects for Democracy
in the United States of America 19**

Chapter Four: American Democracy in Practice. 21

Chapter Five: The Power and The Peril of the
Idea of American Exceptionalism. 29

Chapter Six: America's Love-Hate Relationship with Government,
and its Consequences 37

Chapter Seven: Low Voter Turnout and Engagement. 43

Chapter Eight: Gridlock In Washington and the States:
Causes and Consequences 49

Chapter Nine: Foreign Policy 55

Chapter Ten: Dueling Economic Approaches .61

PART III: **Moving The Political System of The United States
Toward Democracy 67**

Chapter Eleven: Summarizing the Malaise of American Democracy 69

Chapter Twelve: A Modest Catalogue of Democratic Reforms 75

Chapter Thirteen: Political Literacy:
A critical Prerequisite to Viable Democracy. 81

Chapter Fourteen: Restoring Majority Rule in Congress 87

Chapter Fifteen: Reforming the Executive Branch 91

Chapter Sixteen: The Federal Judicial System and Democracy 99

Chapter Seventeen: Democracy and Elections in the United States. 105

Chapter Eighteen: Improving U.S. Elections: Increasing Participation,
Lowering Costsand Securing Results. 111

Chapter Nineteen: Moving Towards the Tricentennial
                       Creating a 21st Century Democratic America
                       with a Democratic Reform Agenda 119

Chapter Twenty: Proportional Representation: Pros and Cons 127

Chapter Twenty-One: How To Democratize
                       the American Political System 133

About The Author. 141

Index. 143

Preface

America is in a political crisis. Its once-great political system is coming closer and closer to outright failure and an inability to meet the governing needs of the nation. The current 112th Congress has been the least productive in history and we have to go back to the War Between the States to find a Congress that has been more contentious and less civil. According to a June, 2014 Gallup Poll, confidence in all of the branches of the federal government continues to plunge and is at its lowest point since this polling series was started in 1991.

This book is my attempt to distill what I have learned in my more than fifty years of studying, teaching, and writing about politics and government, to ask what needs to be done to restore the American political system, and to offer some workable answers and solutions.

This is not written as an academic tome (although I have written several of these over the years). Instead, it is a call to action that is aimed at the active—not necessarily activist—citizens among us who would like to see our political system do better and are willing to consider changes to make that happen.

As a political scientist, journalist, and active citizen (I have worn all three hats at one time or another), I have written this essay out of a dual appreciation for the value of democracy as the best form of government and a sense of patriotism and hope for my native land, the United States of America. My working hypothesis is that the slow decline over the last quarter of a century or more of the United States as a great nation and the preeminent moral leader of the globe is not irreversible. Indeed, the decline could be halted and even reversed if the United States shook off the shackles of oligarchy by embracing more democracy.

"Change is the law of life. And those who look only to the past or present are certain to miss the future."

—John F. Kennedy

Democracy is probably the most significant and practical form of government that has been developed over the history of mankind. Because it is a simple but far-reaching way of allowing those who are ruled by government to have a say in decisions that affect them, democracy is imbued with a moral legitimacy that few, if any, competing forms of government enjoy.

What is democracy? At its basis, it is self-government. In small societies and possibly in large societies in the future, given the rapid and steady development of modern communications technology, it is a "town-meeting" style of government where the citizens rule directly. The citizens hire and provide marching orders to administrators who have little policy discretion. In most modern nation states today, though, it has evolved into a form of government that we call indirect democracy. In the latter, people do not rule directly but, instead, (s)elect their rulers and hold them responsive to public opinion through an electoral mechanism that provides for a finite term of office, at the end of which the electorate can either re-elect (and thereby ratify) those in power, or throw them out and replace them with those who pledge different policies.

Despite this appearance of simplicity, many continue to debate the precise meaning and boundaries of democracy. For purposes of this analysis, I have adopted a definition that is fairly straightforward…rule by the people rather than for the people, whether directly or indirectly.

The origins of the term tell us quite a bit about its meaning. It comes from two Greek words, *demos* and *kratia*. Demos is generally translated into English as "the people" and kratia means "power" or "government." In modern English, that translates simply to self-government.

Through the writings of Thucydides, Plato, Aristotle, and what we can infer about the actions of Athenian leaders such as Solon and Pericles, we know that it was the guiding principle of government in the ancient city-state of Athens dating from around 500 BCE. While the Athenians embraced the principles of democracy, they did not fully follow them in practice since their democratic assemblies excluded women, foreigners, and slaves. Only about one in five adults were fully enfranchised.

In the succeeding 25 centuries, democracy has undergone significant changes and has been championed by a long line of Western political thinkers such as Jean Jacques Rousseau, John Locke, Jeremy Bentham, John Stuart Mill and many more. The preponderance of the changes were, and are, adaptations of democracy to the modern densely-populated nation-state, pushing it toward representative rather that direct democracy. Democracy has also become associated with the political value of equality which has led to the enfranchisement of all adults regardless of sex or property status.

Despite its many advantages, a thorough and objective analysis of democracy requires us to be honest about what it is and is not. Democracy is a moral and legitimate way of determining who gets what, when, and how. What it is not is a form of government without faults. Chief among these is that it is relatively inefficient and slow to move compared to oligarchies because it takes time for issues to work their way through the citizenry and to articulate and aggregate public opinion into public policy. Oligarchies can move far more swiftly, albeit at a price in the restriction of liberty. Some also point to demagoguery and manipulation of public opinion as important faults. Perhaps they are, but a reading of history demonstrates that democracies are no more (and perhaps less) prone to this than oligarchies.

The recognition of the faults of democracy was the motivation for the oft-quoted Winston Churchill statement, delivered in a House of Commons on Nov. 11, 1947, that, "Democracy is the worst form of government, except for all those other forms that have been tried from time to time." He was right. Democracies do indeed make mistakes and take wrong courses, but they correct them faster and more often than any other form of government.

Author Beliefs

I feel that I owe it to you as a reader to reveal my ideas and influences and beseech you to examine your own beliefs and the extent you use them as filters to accept or reject the ideas of others. My beliefs surely influence my ideas, but I strive as a trained social scientist and human being to be as objective as possible and not let my beliefs get in the way of objective conclusions, factual descriptions, or to color my policy recommendations. I leave it to others to determine the extent to which I have succeeded in this quest.

To begin, I call myself a liberal democrat because I have a deep commitment to liberty (the root of liberalism over the centuries of its evolution) and am also a believer in democracy as an effective and morally sufficient way of governing.

As a political scientist who majored in political science during the achievement of three degrees, and as a college professor for 25 years, I had the opportunity to read and write extensively on the subject of democratic political thought and American politics. I taught several score of basic sections of American Government as well as many advanced courses on American political thought and the history of European political thought. Each basic course I taught was organized around the questions of what democracy is, to what extent is the America political system is democratic, and why any of that might matter. During that quarter-century career, perhaps either as a function of my maturity as a political scientist or the impact of the ideas and viewpoints of literally thousands of students and many colleagues, or more probably, as a function of both, my ideas about democracy in the United States developed and are reflected in this work.

My ideas have also been influenced by my direct participation in the political system. I was a major-party candidate for public office when I ran against a seven-term incumbent in the United States House of Representatives. I lost the election, although I did win over 55,000 votes and a deep appreciation for what candidates (particularly those without huge campaign war chests) face during a campaign. Also influential has been my experience over 40 years of being a political party volunteer, a campaign manager for several local candidates, and as a public opinion pollster.

Methodology and Conclusions

This book is primarily a vehicle for my political philosophy and policy recommendations, and is an expression of long-form journalism more than it is a scholarly publication. It was originally penned as a 19-part essay that appeared in *Living On The Suncoast* Magazine, a lifestyle magazine based in greater Sarasota, Florida, that I own and publish. It is intended as a journalistic undertaking and call to action rather than as a traditional scholarly analysis replete with citations and footnotes, though intellectual honesty compels me to cite sources when relevant. As an essay-based book, it emulates the long tradition of normative political thought as writing that advocates as much as it analyzes.

My conclusions are fairly simple: while I offer anecdotal evidence rather than comprehensive surveys or scientific evidence in support of my conclusions, it is my judgment that Americans as a whole are unfamiliar with democracy both in principle and to what extent it operates in their political system, and are politically impoverished as a result. The anecdotal evidence I present is what I have gleaned from decades of monitoring media treatment of the subject of how democracy is treated in the many high school Civics texts I have read, from discussions with hundreds of college students in American Government courses, and my analysis of the utterings on the topic by public officials and candidates for public office. Based on that, I conclude that we falsely assume that the United States of America is the epitome of democracy. As a result, serious discussions of democracy in the United States is absent from American politics, political culture, and public policy proposals. Furthermore, I suggest that this ignorance and complacency lead to unexamined and often-costly policy implications and weaken us as a political system. As a remedy for this, I advocate more democracy.

Acknowledgements

I owe a debt of gratitude to my wife Virginia's unflagging encouragement and support in producing this work, despite her knowledge as the Chief Financial Officer of the magazine that we jointly own that the space devoted to originally publishing the essays could have been devoted to profitable content instead.

I also acknowledge the wisdom and patient teaching of my political science professors during my undergraduate work at Ohio State University and, especially, during my graduate work at the University of Wisconsin-Madison. My professor and co-author Robert Booth Fowler has been especially influential.

Thanks also to Veronica Belmont for her through editing and to Barbara Dee for her technical assistance in preparing this manuscript for publication in paper and electronic form.

PART I:

Democracy

Although our interests as citizens vary, each one is an artery to the heart that pumps life through the body politic, and each is important to the health of democracy.

Democracy works when people claim it as their own

BILL MOYERS, *The Nation*, Jan. 22, 2007

1

Chapter One

Democracy: An Enduring Political Ideal and Practice

Democracy In Principle

In order to evaluate the accuracy of the widely-held American belief that the U.S. A. is the epitome of democracy, we need to understand what democracy is and how it has developed historically. The best way to do this is to consult the long tradition of Western political thought because democracy has been a central topic within that venerable and significant literature. Significantly, the democratic thinkers and advocates within that literature have inspired nation-builders across the centuries to adopt their ideas in the constitutions they have built. The very word *democracy*, as well as its institutions, has stirred passion and debate for millennia. Over the span of written political thought, from the ancestors of the ancient Greeks to contemporary political theorists, a large, eclectic and influential coterie of political thinkers and government analysts and activists have defined, debated, vilified and celebrated democracy.

Turning first to a literal meaning of democracy, its etymological origins date to the classical era of Greece, although Greek political thinkers of the era referred to the democratic ideas of those that came before them. The modern term democracy is a combination of two Greek words, *demos* and *kratia*. In the context of what we know of Greek government through Thucydides, Plato and others, intellectuals and policy makers of the day used the term to mean the literal vesting of political power in the citizenry of the city-state, the main form of political organization of the era. Citizenship, however, was far from universal at the time. Athens excluded women and slaves from enfranchisement. Nevertheless, despite this shortcoming, the Greek system was known as participatory or direct democracy, a political system where people literally govern themselves.

Thucydides, an Athenian general and author of the History of the *Peloponnesian War*, was not a huge fan of democracy because he thought it was not compatible with military efficiency. Still, as a loyal Athenian, he defined and defended it in the Funeral Oration he wrote in Pericles' voice. He quotes the Athenian democratic leader saying that Democracy allows men to advance because of merit instead of wealth or inherited class. It fosters lawful behavior, freedom, and privacy, and provides equal justice for all as they settle private disputes.

Thucydides writes: "Our constitution …favors the many instead of the few; this is why it is called a democracy. If we look to the laws, they afford equal justice to all in their private differences; if no social standing, advancement in public life falls to reputation for capacity, class considerations not being allowed to interfere with merit; nor again does poverty bar the way, if a man is able to serve the state, he is not hindered by the obscurity of his condition. The freedom which we enjoy in our government extends also to our ordinary life….we do not feel called upon to be angry with our neighbor for doing what he likes, or even to indulge in those injurious looks which cannot fail to be offensive…But all this ease in our private relations does not make us lawless as citizens. Against this fear is our chief safeguard, teaching us to obey the magistrates and the laws, particularly such as regard the protection of the injured, whether they are actually on the statute book, or belong to that code which, although unwritten, yet cannot be broken without acknowledged disgrace."

These attitudes took root in Western democratic thought and culture. Hence, they do not sound terribly different than the democratic ideals espoused at patriotic holiday celebrations in contemporary Europe and North America.

As I wrote in *An introduction to Political Theory: Toward The Next Century*, a book I co-authored with Robert Booth Fowler (New York: Harper-Collins College Publishers, 1993), "Even though those who value democracy-known as democrats-do not think exactly alike. They share a belief in many principles which are reflected in the literature of political theory. Very prominent among these is the idea that citizens are morally entitled to band together with their neighbors to speak out on the issues of the day and to attempt to convince a majority of their fellow citizens… in what English political theorist John Stuart Mill referred to as the free marketplace of ideas….All serious democrats also share the conviction that citizens have a moral right and a collective, if not individual, capacity to pick the rulers, if not the policies, of government….It is a matter of simple arithmetic: To fail to pursue democracy is to allow the few to tell the many what to do….In addition, all good democrats feel compelled to abide by the outcome of a democratic process regardless of how personally distasteful the results may be…because the process itself is intrinsically valuable."

4

Fowler and I also point out that democratic cultural norms, while popular, are also very fragile until they have taken firm root over generations, if not centuries. With the institutionalization of a strong cultural commitment to play by the rules, democracy becomes less fragile and can withstand attempts by despots to overthrow it because people in a firmly-rooted democratic culture tend to support democratic systems despite personal risk and long odds against success. They value the moral and practical benefits of self-government and are willing to fight for them.

Another important issue faced by all democratic political systems and ideas involves limitations on the majorities and the rights afforded to all. In democratic systems, freedom of speech, press, and assembly are held to be sacred and cannot be proscribed even by a decision of the majority because they are necessary for the system to function. In order for a free marketplace of ideas to exist, merchants of all ideas and policies have to be able to offer their wares to shoppers, so to speak. It is the only way fringe ideas can hope to garner a majority or even the respect of a significant minority. Campaign laws that restrict access to the marketplace of ideas to those with massive funds are not free in any sense of the word and are, therefore, not democratic.

Democracy is not just a Western idea. As Deigo Von Vacaano, a political theorist at Texas A&M University, blogged in the Washington Post on January 8, 2014, people in places all over the globe have democratic aspirations. He writes, "Events in Turkey, Egypt, Brazil and North Korea have strained …faith in democracy." He cites several corruption scandals and dictatorships as reasons to "…ask whether democracy, and especially liberal democracy, is simply a Western value that cannot take root in other cultures." He suggests it is not, and cites writings in Islamic thought that popular sovereignty is authorized concretely by God's law, or divine and popular sovereignty are fused and are made manifest in the world through each other. He also cites in Chinese political thought that equality and inequality were relevant instrumentally to some of Confucianism's key social and political concerns. His conclusion is that while both the intellectual underpinnings of political theory and the institutional history of non-western states make democracy and liberty play out differently, they are still powerful concepts that drive democratic aspirations and institutions around the globe, not just in Europe or North America.

Across the broad sweep of history, democracy refuses to die, despite centuries of authoritarian and totalitarian challenges to democratic political systems and ideals. It has become a perennial topic of political thought worldwide. Virtually every serious political thinker is compelled to discuss democracy, whether as proponents or opponents. It is also a politically potent ideal that remains immensely popular, manifesting itself in such disparate movements as Occupy Wall Street and the "Arab Spring" as well as leading to the holding of elections (whether truly democratic elections or not) around the world in nations that are generally not considered to be democratic. It is such a significant and politically-charged idea that almost every despot and authoritarian regime tries to legitimize itself by claiming to be democratic, however "guided" that democracy might be.

As a "living" tradition and practice, democratic theory and governmental practice have evolved considerably over the centuries since Pericles, paralleling (if not responding to) the development of the densely-populated nation-state and modern communications and transportation infrastructure along the way. While democrats everywhere share a commitment and understanding of the general norms of democracy, they diverge on the form that they think democracy should take.

> *The good news, to relieve all this gloom, is that a democracy is inherently self-correcting. Here, the people are sovereign. Inept political leaders can be replaced. Foolish policies can be changed. Disastrous mistakes can be reversed.*
>
> —Theodore C. Sorensen

Forms of Democratic Practice

Concurrent with the rise of the nation-state and widespread public education and mass communications, democracy in the modern era has evolved into two major forms—the direct or participatory democracy practiced by the Athenians, and indirect or representative democracy.

Direct democracy is a straightforward concept: those adults who are affected by government have the right to debate and vote upon governmental decisions.

Representative democracy, on the other hand, while fairly straightforward in principle, is more nuanced and varied in practice since it has evolved in several institutional variations. As nation-states with large populations emerged over the long run of Western history and political thought, many democratic theorists suggested democracy was too unwieldy to involve everyone directly. Instead, its proponents thought its ideals could still be realized in a governmental system where the people do not rule directly but rule indirectly by electing the government and holding it responsive to public opinion through the threat or removal of the government in a general election. The common term for this is *indirect* or *representative* democracy, and it evolved in Europe and culminated in the parliamentary system that was born in the English Reform Act of 1832, following the ideas of Locke and other British political theorists. Emulating the stable English model and British colonial influence, a significant number of contemporary representative democracies are parliamentary systems in which the voters elect the legislature and the party that controls the legislative majority appoints the executive who is, in turn, responsible to the appointing body. The executive can be removed by legislators in a vote of no confidence, or by the voters who can elect a different majority at the next election.

A presidential variation of representative democracy has evolved as well. It is characterized by a separation of powers between the executive and legislative functions of government and, usually, separate elections for both of them. Another close variation is the *democratic monarchy* where the executive power is invested in an appointed (sometimes hereditary) individual, although for the system to be truly democratic, the monarch or head of state is considered a figurehead and is not given significant policy responsibilities.

No matter which form is followed by representative democratic practice, voters force policy makers to respond to public opinion through elections where voters can either re-elect the government or throw it out and replace it. Critical to this process is the necessity of general elections. In modern representative democracies, general elections are the means by which all adults (except for resident aliens) have an inalienable right and opportunity to vote "yea" or "nay" on the entire government in a given election; therefore, when a majority of voters cast votes to change the government, it is changed completely and swiftly. An incentive is thereby created for the government to act in the peoples' interest in order to get re-elected.

Chapter Two

Democracy In America:
Alexis de Tocqueville's Vision and Influence

In the following sections, we will examine the precise nature of democracy and the role that general elections play in it, where we stand as a nation relative to other nations on a variety of indexes (including an index or measure of democracy), and evaluate how the level and nature of American democracy affects outcomes and policies.

We will also try to analyze how we got to where we are as a nation and attempt to define some of the major problems and challenges we face, e.g., we will speculate on the causes for some of our challenges and what seems to make sense to do about meeting them with an infusion of democracy into the nation's constitution. In other words, I am not content to simply analyze but, in the tradition of normative political theory, will also prescribe and offer ideas for both short-range and long-range solutions to the national dilemmas and problems.

Democracy and socialism have nothing in common but one word, equality. But notice the difference: while democracy seeks equality in liberty, socialism seeks equality in restraint and servitude.

—Alexis de Tocqueville

Although not as influential as the ideas of the founding generation of the political system of the United States of America, the ideas of Alexis de Tocqueville have been influential in the evolution of American democratic thought. In 1831, a scant 31 years after the U.S. Constitution was finished, French social and political analysts Alexis de Tocqueville and Gustave de Beaumont were sent to the United States by the French government to study the American prison system. When they got here, they decided to expand their analysis to American society and its experiences with democracy. Their wanderings around the new and rapidly-growing nation culminated in de Tocqueville's influential two-volume book called *Democracy in America*, published in 1835 and 1840. Within its pages, he examined how the worldwide democratic revolution that he believed had evolved over the past seven centuries was faring in America.

9

His analysis makes the claim that a republican (non-monarchical) and representative form of democracy had taken root in the United States even though it had failed in so many other places because of the optimistic and egalitarian spirit of American political culture.

He assesses the future of democracy in the United States through an analysis of likely threats *to* democracy and its possible dangers. He posits that democracy has a tendency to degenerate into "soft despotism" and emphasizes the risk of developing a tyranny of the majority that threatens the rights of the minority. He also notes that religion plays a strong role in the rapid development of the United States, and posits that the reason was due to the separation of church and state, thereby bypassing the antagonism between democracy and religion and allowing energy to go into nation-building.

Despite the glowing report of the state of American politics, government, and society in *Democracy in America*, political scientist Aurelian Craiutu showed in his book *Tocqueville on America after 1840: Letters and Other Writings*, (Cambridge, Cambridge University Press, 2009), that de Tocqueville became disillusioned with the United States after 1840. His letters to friends showed that he increasingly disapproved of the direction that the United States was taking because of political corruption, slavery, territorial expansionism, and the encroachment of the economic sphere upon the political.

De Tocqueville was correct and even quite prescient in predicting the violent clash that would arise over slavery, the rise of an industrial oligarchy, and the emergence of the U.S.A. as a superpower and international rival for power and influence. Nevertheless, his analysis also had some significant shortcomings.

He predicted wrongly that equality in America would stifle the development of a literary tradition and he predicted that the U.S. would remain a scientific backwater. Most importantly in this context, the aristocratic de Tocqueville dwelled at length on the power of majority to carry the day in a democracy, calling it a "tyranny of the majority." He was sympathetic to limiting it with minority rights that could prevent majorities from ruling. This has been thoroughly inculcated into contemporary American democracy with its requirements for supermajorities, term limits, and other roadblocks to democracy which go far beyond the need for civil liberties and the freedom of speech, press, and assembly that are necessary to ensure democratic stability.

Despite the shortcomings of de Tocqueville's analyses, his perspectives on the political system raised some important issues about democracy in America and they are among those that we will be examining in this book.

Following de Tocqueville's tradition of self-examination, I will attempt to explore the often-opaque and complex issues that surround whether the U.S.A. is a democratic nation, and what that means for our citizens and public policies.

Chapter Three

Democracy, Republic or Hybrid:
The Founders' Republicanism

"I pledge allegiance to the flag of the United States of America, and to the republic for which it stands…" These familiar words, written by Baptist Minister Francis Bellamy in 1882, memorized by almost every school child in the United States of America and repeated at civic functions throughout life, are not merely a ritualistic patriotic phrase. They describe one of the most fundamental characteristics of the American political system. The United States is a republic and not a democracy.

Basic Civics Definitions

The term *republic*, widely used but little understood in American political discourse, was a term used by 18th century political thinkers describing a form of government without a monarchy. In a republic, public affairs are considered a "public matter" (Latin: *res publica*), instead of the private property of hereditary monarchs, dictators, or emperors.

Today, political scientists seldom use it because it has little explanatory or descriptive power. But when they do, they use it to classify governments where the head of state is not a monarch. It applies to such diverse nations as the U.S.A., China, Russia, and North Korea which have little in common governmentally. Interestingly, it does not describe democracies like the United Kingdom, Japan, or Belgium because they have a hereditary, if largely ceremonial, head of state.

To the extent that they think about the institutional characteristics of the U.S. political system, most Americans think the U.S.A. is a democracy as well as a republic. It is *not* a democracy but it *is* a republic. More precisely, American government is a hybrid form of government with democratic elements. As we have seen, democracy means *rule of the people* and describes a political system where people govern themselves (direct or participatory democracy), such as in a New England-style town meeting, or where the people do not rule directly but elect the government and hold them responsive to public opinion through the threat of removing the government in a general election (indirect or representative democracy).

Most modern representative democracies are parliamentary systems where the legislature is the supreme body and is elected directly, and the party that controls the majority appoints the executive who is responsible to the appointing body and can be removed by legislators in a vote of no confidence.

The U.S.A. is certainly not governed by a huge town meeting or online referendum (although New England Town Meetings still persist and people are asked to vote on state and local policy referenda from time to time), so it is not a direct democracy. It does not qualify as a representative democracy either because of staggered elections. We elect an independent president (with veto power) every four years, one third of the Senate every two years, all of the House of Representatives every two years, and never elect the judiciary which is appointed for life.

The critical principle at issue here is that the American people can never exercise their franchise to elect or un-elect a whole government, which is a requirement for indirect democracy and an incentive for government adherence to public opinion. We are always voting but seldom change things in a fundamental manner by our votes.

Clearly, as we have seen, this is what the U.S. founders wanted. While most of them opposed a monarch because of their bad experiences with the British Crown, they also feared democracy. Democracy was not mentioned in the Declaration of Independence or the constitution by deliberate omission. The founders were familiar with democratic principles and rejected them. When they assembled in Philadelphia in 1787, they had a blank governmental drawing board. It was well within their power to adopt a democratic constitution but they choose not to. Instead, they developed an elaborate system of federalism (giving states power in some areas), checks, balances and protections against majority opinion that allowed voting for a part of the government by a white male minority but avoided truly general elections. It was not until later in U.S. history that the Senate was elected directly (albeit one third at a time), and it took a civil war to enfranchise black males—and women did not get to vote until the 20th century.

Illustrating these points in the founders' own words, Benjamin Franklin, when asked what form of government had been created in the new Constitutional Convention, replied, "A republic, if you can keep it."

On May 31,1787, Edmund Randolph told his fellow Constitutional Convention delegates that the goal was "to provide a cure for the evils under which the United States labored; that in tracing these evils to their origin every man had found it in the turbulence and trials of democracy..." (referring to the Articles of Confederation).

Another delegate, Elbridge Gerry (who gave gerrymandering its name), said: "The evils we experience flow from the excess of democracy. The people do not want (that is, do not lack) virtue; but are the dupes of pretended patriots."

On June 21, 1788, Alexander Hamilton stated in a speech that "The ancient democracies in which the people themselves deliberated never possessed one good feature of government. Their very character was tyranny; their figure deformity..." Another time Hamilton said: "We are a Republican Government. Real liberty is never found in despotism or in the extremes of Democracy."

Samuel Adams warned: "Remember, Democracy never lasts long. It soon wastes, exhausts,

and murders itself! There never was a democracy that 'did not commit suicide.'"

James Madison wrote, "...democracies have ever been spectacles of turbulence and contention; have ever been found incompatible with personal security, or the rights of property; and have in general been as short in their lives as they have been violent in their deaths."

In Federalist #10 he wrote, "A republic is different from a democracy because its government is placed in the hands of delegates...in a republic, the delegates both filter and refine the many demands of the people so as to prevent the type of frivolous claims that impede purely democratic governments."

In Republics, the great danger is, that the majority may not sufficiently respect the rights of the minority.

—James Madison

Evolution and Some Implications

The political system the U.S.A. has today has evolved in many ways from what the founders envisioned. In terms of citizen enfranchisement, the system is now far more inclusive since race, sex, and property ownership have been abolished as legal voting criteria, although the federal government still has the need to enforce the Voting Rights Act against all-too-frequent state and local efforts to suppress voter turnout for partisan advantage and to keep the existing elites in power.

Moreover, states regularly engage in gerrymandering (fixing district boundaries to favor the party in power) which perpetuates the continued rule of those already in office, whether currently representing a majority or not. For example, Florida has a slim majority of Democrats and voted for Barack Obama for President in 2008 and 2012 while simultaneously electing lopsided majorities of Republicans in the state legislature due to districts drawn to strongly favor incumbents.

Also, the dominance of commercial media as information sources, particular television, has provided a huge entrée for monied interests to provide huge campaign contributions for legislators and executives who favor their positions, and gain influence and policy support in the process.

In this environment, public opinion has a difficult time gaining influence. It must be very strong, consistent, and loud for a long time before its effect is felt on policy makers and pressures them to override the influence of special interests. In principle, as few as five Supreme Court justices, 41 Senators (under current rules), or 218 members of the House of Representatives (or, effectively, a key Congressional committee chair) can stop the process.

A quick bit of political arithmetic handily illustrates the point. In order to enact a law in the U.S. government (and most states as well), a concurrent majority is needed in both houses of Congress (60% in the Senate according to its self-adopted rules, except for Presidential nomination confirmations which were reduced to a true majority by Senate rules in 2014). The President must agree also in most circumstances because, if he vetoes a piece of legislation, it can be overridden only by two thirds of both houses of Congress, a rare occurrence. And the judiciary must concur too if the issue is challenged in the courts.

When we do the math, we find 435 members of the House of Representatives, 100 Senators, nine Supreme Court Justices and one President, constitute a total of 545 constitutionally-empowered national policy makers. Under the separation of powers system, a majority of each must concur for something to work its way through the system. Somebody or some interest group trying to prevent legislation only needs to influence a tiny minority of the government to prevent what they oppose from happening. They can use this minority leverage to hold the whole political system hostage.

That is precisely what is happening currently as the Tea Party faction in Congress (many elected from safe gerrymandered districts) is wreaking havoc in the House of Representatives and holding the entire government hostage to their demands. They constitute a minority of the house but control the balance of power within the Republican House Caucus and have many incumbents fearful of a primary challenge from the right, made more credible by the 2014 defeat of House Majority Leader Eric Cantor, in a Republican primary by a tea-party backed candidate.

Using the power of a minority magnified many times by the separation of powers system, this relatively small group is able to demand huge federal budget cuts. When they don't get what they want, they use their bloc of votes to obstruct. They refuse to compromise and thereby stall legislation or budgets despite the need for their passage. Although they are a relatively small group that can command serious influence in only one legislative house, they have succeeded in throwing a monkey wrench into the gears and grinding government to a halt.

PART II:

21st Century Problems and Prospects for Democracy in the United States of America

I have no fear that the result of our experiment will be that men may be trusted to govern themselves without a master.

—Thomas Jefferson

Chapter Four

American Democracy in Practice

Democracy in the United States of America

The relationship between democracy and government in the United States of America has long been tentative and sometimes even contradictory. Truly, democracy has been a strong current in the river of American political thought, experience, and political culture. Undoubtedly, the hope for, and pursuit of, democracy have been major contributors to the very popular notion that the U.S. A. is a democratic nation. From the beginnings of the American republic, democratic ideas have persisted and been influential. Unfortunately, despite their persistence and influence, democratic ideas have taken a back seat to other ideas and institutional frameworks.

> *Democracy may not prove in the long run to be as efficient as other forms of government, but it has one saving grace: it allows us to know and say that it isn't.*

—Bill Moyers

Political scientist Michael Parenti, wrote in his essay, *A Constitution for the Few: Looking Back to the Beginning,* (International Endowment for Democracy, www.ifed), "To understand the U.S. political system, it would help to investigate its origins and fundamental structure, beginning with the Constitution. The men who gathered in Philadelphia in 1787 strove to erect a strong central government. They agreed with Adam Smith that government was "instituted for the defense of the rich against the poor." He cites sources that show that by 1760, fewer than five hundred men in five colonial cities controlled most of the commerce, shipping, banking, mining, and manufacturing on the eastern seaboard. In the period from the American Revolution to the Constitutional Convention (1776-1787), the big landowners, merchants, and bankers exercised a strong influence over politico-economic life, often dominating the local newspapers which voiced the ideas and interests of commerce. In twelve of the thirteen states (Pennsylvania excepted), only property-owning white males could vote, probably not more than 10 percent of the total adult population.

21

"The specter of Shays' Rebellion hovered over the delegates who gathered in Philadelphia... They were determined that persons of birth and fortune should control the affairs of the nation and check the 'leveling impulses' of the propertyless multitude who composed 'the majority faction.'"

"To secure the public good and private rights against the danger of such a faction," wrote James Madison in Federalist No. 10, "and at the same time preserve the spirit and form of popular government is then the great object to which our inquiries are directed."

Here Madison touched the heart of the matter: how to keep the "form" and appearance of popular government with only a minimum of the substance; how to construct a government that would win some popular support but would not tamper with the existing class structure—a government strong enough to service the growing needs of an entrepreneurial class while withstanding the democratic egalitarian demands of the popular class.

The framers were of the opinion that democracy was "the worst of all political evils," as Elbridge Gerry put it. For Edmund Randolph, the country's problems were caused by "the turbulence and follies of democracy." Roger Sherman concurred, "The people should have as little to do as may be about the Government." According to Alexander Hamilton, "All communities divide themselves into the few and the many. The first are the rich and the wellborn, the other the mass of the people. . . . The people are turbulent and changing; they seldom judge or determine right." He recommended a strong centralized state power to "check the imprudence of democracy." And George Washington, the presiding officer at the Philadelphia Convention, urged the delegates not to produce a document "merely to please the people."

Parenti further argues that, "In keeping with their desire to contain the propertyless majority, the founders inserted what Madison called "auxiliary precautions," designed to fragment power without democratizing it. They separated the executive, legislative, and judicial functions and then provided a system of checks and balances among the various branches, including staggered elections, executive veto, the possibility of overturning the veto with a two thirds majority vote in both houses, Senate confirmation of appointments and ratification of treaties, and a bicameral legislature. They hoped to dilute the impact of popular sentiments. Also, they contrived an elaborate and difficult process for amending the Constitution, requiring proposal by two-thirds of both the Senate and the House, and ratification by three-fourths of the state legislatures. To the extent that it existed at all, the majoritarian principle was tightly locked into a system of minority vetoes, making swift and sweeping popular action less likely.

...Second, not only must the majority be prevented from finding horizontal cohesion, but its vertical force, its upward thrust upon government, should be blunted by interjecting indirect forms of representation. Thus, the senators from each state were to be elected by their respective state legislatures rather than directly by the voters. The chief executive was to be selected by an electoral college elected by the people but, as anticipated by the framers, composed of political leaders and men of substance who months later would gather in their various states and choose a president of their own liking. It was believed that they would usually be unable to muster a majority for any one candidate, and that the final selection would be left to the House, with each state delegation therein having only one vote.

In sum, the Constitution was consciously designed as a conservative document, elaborately equipped with a system of minority locks and dams in order to resist the pressure of popular tides."

But the case is not that one sided, even for Parenti. He underscores the American ambivalence toward democracy in the same essay when he writes, "For all its undemocratic aspects, the Constitution was not without its historically progressive features. Consider the following:

▶ The very existence of a written constitution with specifically limited powers represented an advance over more autocratic forms of government.

▶ No property qualifications were required for any federal officeholder, unlike in England and most of the states. And salaries were provided for all officials, thus rejecting the common practice of treating public office as a voluntary service that only the rich could afford.

▶ The president and legislators were elected for limited terms. No one could claim a lifelong tenure on any elective office

(editor's note: election for a finite term is not the same as term limits which limits the number of terms that can be won by an office holder.)

▶ Article VI reads: "no religious Test shall ever be required as a Qualification to any Office or public Trust under the United States," a feature that represented a distinct advance over a number of state constitutions that banned Catholics, Jews, and nonbelievers from holding office.

▶ Bills of attainder, the practice of declaring by legislative fiat a specific person or group of people guilty of an offense, without benefit of a trial, were made unconstitutional. Also outlawed were ex post facto laws, the practice of declaring some act to be a crime, then punishing those who had committed it before it was made unlawful.

▶ There was strong popular sentiment for a Bill of Rights. In order to assure ratification, supporters of the new Constitution pledged the swift adoption of such a bill as a condition for ratification. So, in the first session of Congress, the first ten amendments were swiftly passed and then adopted by the states; these rights included freedom of speech and religion; freedom to assemble peaceably and to petition for redress of grievances; the right to keep arms; freedom from unreasonable searches and seizures; freedom from self-incrimination, double jeopardy, cruel and unusual punishment, and excessive bail and fines; the right to a fair and impartial trial; and other forms of due process.

▶ The Bill of Rights also prohibited Congress from giving state support to any religion. Religion was to be something apart from government, supported only by its own constituents and not by the taxpayer—a stricture that often has been violated in practice."

Following Parenti's advice to look at the origins of the U.S. political system in order to understand it, I observe a fundamental ambiguity toward democracy in America on the part of citizens of the time as well as the constitution writers. On the one hand, drawing on their perceptions of direct democracy in Athens and in some Swiss cantons and their desire for self-government, early New England settlers from Europe developed a participatory form of local decision making which culminated in a fairly widespread practice of annual town meetings in which the assembled citizens made the town's laws. This tradition of New England-style town meetings still survives in some local governments in the region, albeit with the modern imposition of city managers and other administrative devices. It also re-surfaced in the Progressive movement of the early 20th century and led to many local and state limitations on centralized power.

However, despite the prevalence of New England town meetings in early U.S. history and the strength of the Progressive movement, it is clear from a reading of the historical record that the philosophical soil of the colonies was far more hospitable to republicanism than democracy. To the extent that the emerging political culture reflected a democratic bent rather than being purely republican in eschewing a monarchy, it tended to embrace the presidential form of representative democracy. A plausible explanation lies in the founders' experiences as colonial subjects. Their bad experiences under the British caused them to steer away from monarchy and led them to adopt a form of indirect presidential representative democracy as a conservative alternative to direct democracy or straightforward representative democracy. Along with this, and undoubtedly stemming from the same colonial experiences, they promoted a strong set of civil liberties that ensured minority rights since they distrusted majorities and feared them economically and politically.

The U.S. Constitution, as originally adopted, reflected this ambiguity, although a good case can be made that, in the main, it tilted against democracy. The original document incorporated the straightforward democratic elements of the direct election of the U.S. House of Representatives. Balancing this was the indirect election of the President and the Senate and the enfranchisement of only propertied white males. The democratic currents in U.S. political culture have led us to enfranchise all adults and elect the Senate directly, although the indirect election of the President still is the case, since the Electoral College is more than an historical artifact and has, indeed, led to awarding the office to a candidate who actually received fewer votes than his opponent four times, in the 1824 selection of John Quincy Adams, the 1876 selection of Rutherford B. Hayes, the 1888 selection of Benjamin Harrison, and the 2000 selection of George W. Bush.

The Constitution of the United States of America was not penned as a democratic document. Article IV Section 4 of the Constitution states: "The United States shall guarantee to every State in this Union a Republican form of Government." As understood by political scientists, this means a government that is not a monarchy or dictatorship, but not necessarily a democracy. The founders of this nation wanted to free themselves from the British monarchy but did not intend to turn significant power over to the citizens. Neither the Declaration of Independence nor the Constitution even mention democracy. In fact, the founders' writings make it abundantly clear that they feared giving too much power to the people, the major reason why they created a constitutional system of separation of powers and checks and balances system that is designed (and works) to prevent general elections. Americans cannot vote to change (or re-elect) the entire government in one election or even in a series of elections.

The present constitution (as amended over the years) allows Americans to vote for the House of Representatives every two years, but we vote only indirectly (given the electoral college) for the President every other election. We also vote for only one third of the Senate at a time (originally, the founders had the state legislatures appoint Senators) and we never vote for the federal judiciary. Frequently, we are left with a divided government with a different party (and a majority from a different election) holding each house and/or a Congress controlled by one party and the White House controlled by another. While this is firmly entrenched as desirable in the American civic ethic, it is also a recipe for gridlock and frustration of majority opinion. No matter how united on a cause the U.S. electorate may be, most of the government remains untouched and the will of the electorate is not brought to bear in a given national election.

Looking at these numbers, powerful and well-funded interests use this divided government to their advantage by being aware of the de facto veto points in the system and exploiting them to block legislation that they do not like. Toward this end, they concentrate their resources to bankroll and elect just enough sympathetic Senators to stop a majority in that house or support a President who will appoint sympathetic Supreme Court judges, thereby effectively holding the entire political system hostage to their wants. That is much harder to do in a system where it takes an absolute majority of the entire government to block legislative action, such as in a parliamentary system.

As previously mentioned, a profoundly undemocratic element in our system is the Electoral College with its winner-take-all awarding to a candidates who might only win 50.1% of the vote in a given state. Also undemocratic is our campaign finance system and the little-remarked but very significant two-from-each-state apportionment of the Senate which gives people from Wyoming (population 576.412) a staggering 67 times the per-capita representation in the U.S. Senate than California (population 38,041,430), or 33.5 more representation than Florida (population 19,317,568).

A parliamentary system such as is found in Canada, Britain, and much of Europe comes much closer to the representative democratic model than the hybrid model of the U.S.A. Voters in parliamentary systems can, and occasionally do, change their governments at a single election. Moreover, since the executive in a parliamentary system is, by definition, the leader of the majority party, there is no divided government and resulting gridlock that is common in the U.S. The winners have a majority and use it to enact their platform and answer to voters at the next election about the popularity of their policies. In some cases (rare in Canada and England where rules discourage rather than outlaw a proliferation of multiple political parties), no party gets a majority at a general election and the largest vote-getter forms a coalition government.

The conclusion is that, despite beliefs to the contrary, the U.S. has evolved into a hybrid partially-democratic republic and not a representative democracy. The stark reality is that the American people can never go to the ballot box and elect or un-elect a whole government, which is a requirement for indirect democracy and an incentive for government adherence to public opinion. Perhaps low voter turnout is due to the sense (even unconsciously) that voting seldom changes things in a fundamental manner.

Our founders' vision of a checks and balances system that frustrates the will of the majority persists today. We have democratic elements in the system such as the bi-annual election of the entire House of Representatives. We have also abolished property qualifications for voters, enfranchised women and racial minorities, and allowed the direct election of the Senate (albeit, one third at a time). But these laudable reforms have not transformed us into a democracy.

Clearly, the U.S.A. in the 21st century is not governed by a huge town meeting or online referendum (although New England Town Meetings still persist and people are asked to vote on state and local policy referenda from time to time), so it is not a direct democracy. It does not qualify as a representative democracy either because of staggered elections and unevenly apportioned districts. We elect an independent President (with veto power) every four years, one third of the Senate every two years, all of the House of Representatives every two years, and never elect the judiciary which is appointed for life.

Fortunately, our governmental model works for us more often than not because of our history and shared culture. Many who analyze contemporary American culture, journalism, and education observe that it is a fundamental and pervasive civic belief of Americans that the United States is a democracy. Americans also widely believe that American democracy works so well that it constitutes a worthy model for other nations to emulate in their constitutions and government.

However, history has not borne this out. It has not been particularly exportable because of its unique roots in our history, and it is not very often emulated as a form of government by nations with a different culture and history. Moreover, it is an open question whether it works for us in the current environment of mass communication, and whether alternative forms of self-government might serve our nation better.

Understanding how most of the world views democracy and the extent to which the U.S.A. fits that definition is an important task because definitions and the shared cultural understandings that emanate from them have consequences. They color our political and civic expectations of each other and have a significant impact on how our government views and treats us as citizens. They are also important drivers of both domestic and foreign policy and play a role in how we are viewed by other nations as well as how we view them.

Chapter Five

The Power and The Peril of the
Idea of American Exceptionalism

Sizing Up The United States of America As a Nation

Historian Howard Zinn wrote in *American Exceptionalism* (reproduced at www.iefd.org from an original essay *in The Boston Review)* that "The notion of American exceptionalism is not new. It starts as early as 1630 in the Massachusetts Bay colony when Governor John Winthrop utters the words which centuries later would be quoted by Ronald Reagan. Winthrop called the Massachusetts Bay colony a 'city on a hill.' Reagan embellished a little, calling it a 'golden city on a hill.'"

"The idea of a city on a hill is heartwarming. It suggests what ... [presidents] have spoken of: The United States is a beacon of liberty and democracy. People can look to us, and learn from and emulate us.... the idea of American exceptionalism—that the United States alone has the right—whether by divine sanction or moral obligation—to bring civilization, or democracy, or liberty to the rest of the world...finds acceptance on all sides of the political spectrum."

Along with our national belief that we as Americans understand democracy and are the major example of it in the world, deeply engrained in our political culture is the notion that the United States is the greatest country in the world, a world leader in virtually every measure that has any significance. This deeply-seated cultural belief that our nation is unique and exceptional and therefore a leader among nations is not just neutral bragging. It leads us to believe and act upon our belief that the United States of America offers a unique model of freedom that the world can and should follow. This has undoubtedly contributed to interventions in the Middle East, Asia, and elsewhere. As we found out in Iraq, Afghanistan and Viet Nam, among other places, the idea, driven by our blind faith in our exceptionalism and universal appeal, that our brand of freedom and democracy were so desired that the populace of those countries would rush to our side and embrace our ideology was not accurate.

Looking objectively at our relative stance among nations produces a set of facts that our belief in our exceptionalism is not always borne out. On most objective indexes, American leadership is more of a myth than a reality today. We are no longer world leaders in education, standard of living, economic mobility, and a host of other desirable things. Our failure to lead the indexes of comparison among nations in many categories is, in itself, not a cause for alarm and could even be a spur to correcting our deficiencies as a nation. However, our failure to recognize where we stand among the nations of the world has led us to some policy positions and projections of our power, as alluded to above, which have had some less than stellar consequences. While we may have gone into Viet Nam, Iraq, and Afghanistan for other reasons such as containment of cold-war rivals or anti-terrorism, surely our national hubris played a supportive if not a driving role in the decision to intervene in those places, and led us to believe that the outcomes would be different.

Facts vs. Beliefs About American Exceptionalism

Education is a human right with immense power to transform. On its foundation rest the cornerstones of freedom, democracy and sustainable human development.

—Kofi Annan

As a nation, Americans are a proud and patriotic people. Indeed, we have a lot to be proud about.

But, despite repeated assurances by candidates in national elections, several objective statistical measures show the United States is far from number one in many areas that are significant.

In a 2012 report, Todd Leopold of CNN opined, "By a number of objective measures, America is *not* No. 1….Good luck in saying that aloud, however. Forget Social Security. The third rail of American politics is acknowledging we may not be the greatest country in the world." (http://www.cnn.com/2012/07/02/us/american-exceptionalism-other-countries-lessons/index.html)

Some pertinent observations to consider about the idea of American Exceptionalism:

- The U.S.A. indeed does excel at economic freedom, individualism, entrepreneurialism, and technological innovation. We are right to point to ourselves with pride even if we are not in undisputed first place on every index.

- Our higher educational system is beleaguered by budget shortfalls but is still the envy of much of the world. This is not so much true for our K-12 public education anymore.

- Politically, there are at least 15 nations that have substantially more democratic and responsive political systems. Our level of civic knowledge and participation is quite low compared to most other democratic nations.

- Our national infrastructure is in deplorable shape. Our water and sewer systems, electric power grid, and our emergency response capabilities have suffered from budget cuts and deferred maintenance. Many other nations do as well or better. Our transportation infrastructure suffers comparatively and in absolute terms as well because of the same neglect and reluctance to spend. Bridges and freeways are deteriorating at an alarming rate. Our airways system uses obsolete technology, causing delays, fuel wastage and increased risk of collision. Europe, Japan and China have far surpassed us in passenger rail service and high-speed rail systems among city pairs with distances and population densities similar to many potential U.S. routes. American efforts to catch up have been repeatedly stymied by the curious opposition of the right to railroad passenger service.

- On the health front, we lag behind badly. We spend 18% of our gross domestic product on health, far more than most Western nations. Still we rank 49th in life expectancy and 173rd in infant mortality, according to the CIA Factbook. We also have millions of citizens without health insurance and an overburdened emergency medicine system. A system that, in large measure, substitutes for primary and preventive care because many Americans still cannot afford either to pay directly for care or for health insurance, even after the Affordable Care Act of 2013 was passed.

Here are some international indexes from many different sources with many different biases and the ranking the United States on them:

Organization	Name of Ranking	Year	Rank	Out of #
CIA World Factbook	GDP per capita (PPP)	2009	11	227
CIA World Factbook	Life expectancy	2010	49	224
Fund for Peace/ForeignPolicy.com	Failed States Index	2007	168	177
NationMaster	Index of civil and political liberties	2005	7	140
NationMaster	Index of asylum seekers (per capita)	2005	22	28
NationMaster	Index of economic aid (donor, per capita)	2005	19	24
NationMaster	Index of total tax wedge (single worker)	2005	21	29
NationMaster	Index of technological achievement	2005	2	68
New Economics Foundation	Happy Planet Index	2006	114	143
Privacy International	Privacy index (EU and 11 other selected countries)	2006	30	36
Reporters Without Borders	Worldwide Press Freedom Index	2009	20	175
Save the Children	Mother's Index Rank	2007	27	141
Save the Children	Women's Index Rank	2007	22	141
Save the Children	Children's Index Rank	2007	30	141
Save the Children	Percent of seats in the national government held by women	2008	10	177
The Economist Intelligence Unit	e-readiness	2009	5	70
The Economist Intelligence Unit	Index of Democracy	2010	17	167
The Economist Intelligence Unit	Global Peace Index	2010	85	149
The Economist Intelligence Unit	Quality-of-life index	2005	13	111
Transparency International	Corruption Perceptions Index	2008	20	180
United Nations Development Programme	Human Development Index	2010	4	179
United States Patent and Trademark Office	List of patents by country	2007	1	172
Wall Street Journal / The Heritage Foundation	Index of Economic Freedom	2011	9	157
World Bank	Ease of Doing Business Index	2007	3	178
World Economic Forum	Global Competitiveness Report 2010-2011	2010	4	131
World Economic Forum	The Global Gender Gap Report 2007	2007	31	128
World Economic Forum	Enabling Trade Index ranking	2010	19	125
World Health Organization	Suicide rates by country	2005	46	100
Yale University / Columbia University	Environmental Performance Index	2010	61	163

Despite the widespread availability and objectivity of many of these indexes, American public opinion and leadership largely continues to insist on American exceptionalism. The consequences are stark but simple: we tend not to see our problems because we are so certain that we are world leaders in these areas and need no reform. We also often overestimate our power in our foreign policy as a result.

One important consequence of this twin misperception of who we are is that we have disinvested in ourselves while we spend exorbitantly on overseas power projection. In an era of finite budgets, unwillingness to raise taxes, and significant national debt, we do not have the option of funding an ever-expanding defense budget, costly but badly-needed domestic infrastructure renewal, and health care reforms simultaneously. These are but a few of the more controversial issues that have come before the Congress in recent years.

Our hubris and misunderstanding of who we are leads us away from seeking solutions and reforms that can reorient us on a fast track toward self-improvement and regaining leadership in the family of nations.

Subsequent chapters in this book will examine the civic and political dimensions of this in some detail.

So what causes this national hubris and inability to see ourselves as a great nation in certain things, and in dire need of improvement in other things?

Some of it can be traced to garden-variety nationalism. All nations tend to think of themselves as wonderful and superior to others. We are no exception. We may not be number one in jingoism but we are up there in the rankings for certain.

But our history may contribute to this as well. The United States was a clear economic and foreign policy leader among nations after our successes in World War II. We had won the war with an avalanche of industrial production and the successes of our armed forces. We had entered a period of prosperity and growth in the decade after the war ended and we provided aid to rebuild the shattered economies of our former enemies.

We were world leaders in quite a few areas, especially when compared to the devastated economies of Europe and Asia. We also had the political will and the generosity to aid our former enemies in rebuilding their infrastructures after war, thus putting them in a position of strength because they were now reaping the advantages of a new, more efficient infrastructure.

Our belief that we were virtually invincible and number one in virtually everything persisted and even escalated just as the international system changed again and our superiority began to slip. In the aftermath of World War II, an international system emerged that produced another superpower that rivaled us for international influence and led both nations to spend massively on their militaries. While that led to the eventual bankruptcy of the Union of Soviet Socialist Republics and our "victory" in the cold war, it also led us to spend so much on the military sector that our standard of living and infrastructure level dipped in many other areas. Also, as the cold war faded and morphed into a multi-polar international system, guerillas and terrorists who were the sworn enemies of the United States acquired more power. At the same time, technology changed away from favoring large-scale industrial production and thereby allowed small nations to make technological breakthroughs that contributed to their relative rise on many indexes. And now, we are faced with the prospect of the rise of another superpower rival in China. All of these factors contributed to our slippage on many of the indexes of global leadership and power.

While these changes were visible on objective indexes, they were not widely appreciated in our culture; popular belief of our superiority persisted despite evidence to the contrary. While an assessment of the facts today leads to the conclusion that we are still the single most powerful nation on earth, especially in the military arena, we are not all-powerful and unchallengeable in every significant measure of power, influence, and economic prowess. Many nations have surpassed us in such important things as transportation, health care, and standard of living.

A very contributing factor to the policy mistakes that emanate from our hubris is our attitude toward government and the role it plays in successful societies. We don't understand, value, and trust government despite the fact that it created the geo-political environment (and many of the direct institutions) that produced our past abundance and propelled us to greatness. As quoted by the CNN report on the indexes cited above, Craig Wheeland, a Villanova political scientist, traces the national inability to believe that we are not number one to America's innate wariness of government. "We have a peculiar set of approaches to how government should act in our economy and in our society," he says. "That creates a barrier to looking at best practices and borrowing ideas. The business world doesn't think like that. They look at ideas that seem to solve problems and test them out, and if they don't work, they change. They're more pragmatic."

Zinn said, "One of the consequences of American exceptionalism is that the United States government considers itself exempt from legal and moral standards accepted by other nations in the world. There is a long list of such instances: the refusal to sign the Kyoto Treaty regulating the pollution of the environment; the refusal to strengthen the convention on biological weapons. The U.S. has failed to join the hundred or more nations that have agreed to ban land mines, in spite of the appalling statistics on amputations performed on children mutilated by those mines. It refuses to ban the use of napalm and cluster bombs. It insists that it must not be subject, as are other countries, to the jurisdiction of the International Criminal."

Our national hubris and its policy consequences are important parts of our political culture but they do not have to be our destiny. Through a renewed commitment to live up to our potential and a vigorous embracement of democratic government, we can once again become who we would like to be: a world leader and "a city on a hill." One important step along that path would be to become a nation that embarks upon relentless self-education on what democracy is and what it can accomplish for us.

Chapter Six

America's Love-Hate Relationship with Government, and its Consequences

The people of the United States have long had ambivalent and often inconsistent attitudes and practices toward the realm of government and politics. Reflected in what political scientists refer to as American political culture, our national political debate is characterized by a persistent argument, sometimes shrill, sometimes muted, but always present, between those advocates of limited government and those who support government in principle as well as in practice because they see it as a tool for creating a better life. While the Tea Party is the latest iteration of this phenomenon, it has been with us throughout American history and was a major driving force at the 1787 Constitutional Convention.

Because the independent nation of the United States of America was created by fairly well-heeled colonial subjects who chafed under the harsh taxation and often confiscatory policies of British colonialism, their early rhetoric and the Articles of Confederation they drafted were highly critical of concentrated political power and gave a central government very little authority. But the weak and decentralized government they created had major difficulties raising, equipping and feeding a military capable to fight the British. After the war's successful conclusion, the new nation faced an urgent need to knit the former colonies together in commerce and culture. Unfortunately, the original weak government they created proved not to be up to the task.

As Parenti detailed in the previously cited *A Constitution for the Few: Looking Back to the Beginning*, "From colonial times onward, men of influence received vast land grants from the crown and presided over estates that bespoke an impressive munificence. By 1700, three-fourths of the acreage in New York belonged to fewer than a dozen persons. In the interior of Virginia, seven individuals owned over 1.7 million acres. By 1760, fewer than five hundred men in five colonial cities controlled most of the commerce, shipping, banking, mining, and manufacturing on the eastern seaboard. In the period from the American Revolution to the Constitutional Convention (1776-1787), the big landowners, merchants, and bankers exercised a strong influence over politico-economic life, often dominating the local newspapers which voiced the ideas and interests of commerce..."

In twelve of the thirteen states (Pennsylvania excepted), only property-owning white males could vote, probably not more than 10 percent of the total adult population....Not long before the Constitutional Convention, the French chargé d'affaires wrote to his government: Although there are no nobles in America, there is a class of men denominated 'gentlemen.'

In 1787, just such wealthy and powerful 'gentlemen,' our 'founding fathers' (many linked by kinship and business dealings) congregated in Philadelphia for the professed purpose of revising the Articles of Confederation and strengthening the central government."

Because of the obvious and significant failings of America's first limited government and the problems and prospects the new nation faced, even those of the founding elites who were strongly committed to limited government were forced to rethink the original severe limitations on government they had incorporated in the Articles of Confederation. As they gathered in Philadelphia in 1787, they were operating in the environment of a national government that was so weak that it could not levy national taxes. It also required the agreement of at least nine states to act on virtually anything of significance and had little effective power to regulate interstate commerce or build the legal and physical infrastructure needed to grow the economy. Thus, even though the vast majority of the delegates were rich and distrusted government, they felt the strong compulsion to strengthen it—but not too much.

What they created during their deliberations was a constitution that gave a newly-expanded central government substantial powers to erect and maintain a structure of national laws, public order, national defense and public infrastructure, e.g., education, transportation, a postal system, etc., thereby allowing commerce to flow across former colonial boundaries and thereby creating the conditions for a robust economy to take root.

However, ever-mindful of their recent experiences under colonialism and their philosophical distrust of government and, especially, democracy, the government they created had many built-in checks, balances and other limitations on its power that would hobble government as often as it empowered it. The founders were aware of rebellious sentiments that persisted in pockets of the citizenry and the notes and writings that emanated from the convention showed that they were especially fearful of those "without substance." They took pains that such people should be prevented from taking over the government at the ballot box through democratic institutions, lest they use that power to radically redistribute income and power and thereby threaten the privileged position that elites had established for themselves through the separation of powers, and the checks and balances in the new constitution.

Thus, the debate between anti-government libertarians (today's so-called conservatives and Tea Party sympathizers) versus supporters of government as a tool to support the common good was already flourishing in the formative years of the nation. It has intensified and persists into the 21st century with an almost-constant battle between these ideologies, always within the context of a limited ability to change the government via democracy because of the checks and balances built in to prevent such change.

In spite of this, the growing economy and population and the needs of the nation's foreign affairs led to a substantial growth of government and many periods of strong support for government in the military, economic and social investment sectors. The need to fight a civil war, reconstruction, industrialization, two world wars, the depression and other economic setbacks led to the development of a huge, seemingly-permanent military apparatus, a growing regulatory presence to deal with the needs of a complex economy, and a development of a social safety net of pensions and ameliorative programs.

> *Let us never forget that government is ourselves and not an alien power over us. The ultimate rulers of our democracy are not a President and senators and congressmen and government officials, but the voters of this country.*
>
> —Franklin D. Roosevelt

Despite the ideology of limited government, government grew dramatically. But, as it grew, universal support for it did not grow commensurately. To the contrary, most of the expanded government initiatives and programs touched off vehement opposition that swung the ideological pendulum back toward limited government and led to an underfunding, if not the repeal of government programs. The current popularity of the libertarians and Tea Party sympathizers illustrates this well.

These frequent policy pendulum swings are far more than merely interesting debate topics. They have significant consequences. Among these are:

▶ Uncertain funding and on-again-off-again programs complicate planning and discourage investment because investors and governors are unsure of whether support for a program they invest in will continue over the long haul. Current examples are Amtrak and the alternative energy industry. Both have had periods of government support and then saw the rug pulled out from under them. Both persist, although substantially diminished, in the face of opposition because these industries meet important national needs. Neither of them, however, have flourished in the face of budget cuts. Both are unable to meet the needs of the nation in their respective areas and are faced with an uncertain future.

▶ The lack of consistent and predictable subsidies available to U.S. companies puts them at an economic disadvantage. The wide swings of economic and regulatory policy and funding for government assistance programs for American economic enterprise reduce our international competitiveness. Our corporations compete in an economic marketplace against more consistently government-assisted companies in other nations.

▶ Domestically, our distrust of strong national government and our heritage as individual colonies led to our extremely complex and inefficient federal system. America has extensive and duplicative national, state, and local governmental structures. As the U.S. population increased, Americans, driven by the belief that smaller government is more responsive and by the constitutional limitations of national government, formed thousands of duplicative and often-conflicting (and expensive) layers of government.

Currently, there are over 85,000 governments and taxing authorities in the federal system of the United States. Ironically, supporters of a small national government inadvertently become catalysts for increased costs of government because local governments tax and spend to create and administer needed governmental programs locally that are not being handled nationally. This dense patchwork quilt of government is inefficient, costly, and creates both program and departmental duplication and the need for serial support from many layers of government for a given project. That it is why it usually takes a decade or more from idea to fruition for public works projects like roads or bridges.

▶ In such a decentralized system, those with the greatest resources usually get their way. Private interests and local governments who are well-connected can buy media advertising space and thereby gin up public opinion. They often get favored treatment while others get lost in the shuffle as they compete for the favor of policy makers at all levels. Contrary to popular opinion about small government being more responsive to public opinion than large government, it is easier for a large fish in a small pond to get its way than if in a bigger pond. While this supports an entire industry of lobbyists at the national, and especially, at the state and local levels, it also contributes to uneven and inconsistent policies and programs, spotty regulation of the economy, and robust influence of local special interests.

▶ Our historical founders' distrust of government and their creation of our separation of powers system has had some important effects on the democracy that is present within the U.S. political system. As political parties arose and tried to articulate and aggregate public opinion and elect slates of like-minded candidates to government, many who distrust government and politicians have called for primary election systems and term limits to limit the power of political parties and their ability to act as a countervailing influence to other elites. The Progressive movement and the good-government crowd contributed to this with the reforms they advocated that were designed to advance democracy but had the opposite effect: it wound up hobbling political parties which were one of the more effective instruments of democracy because they appealed to and represented the common man. The primary election system that is common in this nation divides political parties and contributes to the high cost of elections. The anti-government former group diminishes the power of those who are elected and, the latter increases the cost of elections. Both further increasing the power of non-elected private interests who fund parties and politicians.

► Our distrust of politics and government also leads to a level of disdain for people who work in or are elected to government. This, coupled with relatively low government salaries compared to equivalent jobs in the private sector, discourages our best and brightest people from pursuing public service careers and contributes to low voter turnout.

Chapter Seven

Low Voter Turnout and Engagement

There is a widespread belief among Americans that citizens should have a say in who is in charge and what is decided by their government. Americans also feel that it is a civic virtue to follow campaigns and vote. Yet, despite this aspect of U.S. political culture and strong encouragement to participate from candidates and political parties, Americans have a shockingly low voter turnout compared to most other democratic or partially-democratic systems. This creates problems and magnifies the power of those who do vote.

For example, the 2013 election for the Sarasota, Florida City Commission resulted in only 17% of the eligible (registered) voters turning out despite newspaper editorials that suggested important public policies were at stake depending on who got elected, widespread and sustained campaign and election coverage in the local newspapers and TV station, and intense online electioneering by several interest groups. Unfortunately, this dismal participation rate is typical for U.S. local elections. According to The GRIO (NBC News) elections for hotly-contested local offices in New York City's 51 districts, "…turnout for elections of this type during the 1980s and 1990s generally ranged between 18 and 23 percent. This pattern is certainly not one limited to New York. Despite its central place in the historic struggle to achieve voting rights for African-Americans, Birmingham, Alabama saw only 20 percent of its registered voters turn out for key city and board of education races on the ballot in August 2013."

While a greater percentage of Americans vote in national elections than turn out for local elections, our performance is nothing to brag about. Our voter turnout still lags dismally behind most nations with public voting. Since 2000, the average Presidential election turnout in the United States has been 55.15% despite ubiquitous campaign commercials and intense "ground game" voter turnout campaigns. This compares to 92% in Austria, 91% in Belgium, 86% in Germany, 85% in Venezuela, 80% in Israel, 74% in Canada and 76% for the House of Commons in the U.K. for similar periods. Also, voter turnout for Congressional elections in Presidential years drops off about 4.1% below these numbers despite the fact that the Congressional races appear on the same ballot (usually right below the

Presidential candidates). Our performance in mid-term Congressional elections, those that take place when the President is not on the ballot, is even worse and reaches an average total of only about 42%.

In terms of engagement, polling data show with consistency that Americans have low levels of confidence in their public officials and do not follow legislation or public policy issues under legislative consideration on a regular basis. The majority of Americans cannot name the majority of the public officials who represent them, nor can they describe the basic outlines of important public policies, much less discuss them perceptively. According to a 2011 Newsweek poll of 1,000 U.S. citizens, 29% could not name the vice president of the United States. 73% couldn't correctly say why we fought the Cold War, 44% were unable to define the Bill of Rights and 6% couldn't circle Independence Day on a calendar.

Causes of Civic Disengagement

While there are many causes of this abysmal level of citizenship engagement, several stand out as particularly important. According to former Senator Robert Graham of Florida, a major cause is the failure of schools to provide even basic civics instruction. Many schools no longer offer civics courses with any substance despite mandates to do so. All too frequently, many teachers assigned to teaching civics are unqualified because they have little or no education in the intricacies of American government and politics and little incentive to acquire it. Additionally, many others have demanding jobs outside of their teaching such as coaching athletic teams and have little time to devote to improving their own civics knowledge.

A functioning, robust democracy requires a healthy educated, participatory followership, and an educated, morally grounded leadership.

—Chinua Achebe

At a minimum, a curriculum of civic education should be taught by qualified individuals who have substantial coursework in university-level political thought, comparative politics and American politics. From a curricular standpoint, it should provide far more than an uncritical description of the institutions and structure of the American political system. A good civic education curriculum should provide a basic understanding of what the institutions are, what they are intended to do and how they perform. It needs to probe some of the major professed political values

44

behind U.S. institutions, (liberty, democracy, justice, equality, economic opportunity, among others), comparatively and objectively explore how U.S. institutions perform relative to other Western industrialized political systems and evaluate if and how they serve citizen needs.

Among the other important contributory causes to poor civic engagement in the U.S. are the presence of staggered elections which necessitate that voters learn the powers and personalities of many levels of public positions, voter fatigue because of a constant parade of national, state and local elections and "bed sheet ballots" which are several pages long and contain arcane and esoteric language describing multiple and often-confusing referenda on policy issues and voting for many obscure offices including judges, law enforcement chiefs, dog catchers, court clerks and so forth.

Another cause of low voter turnout and political participation is the widespread gerrymandering of legislative districts to favor one part over the other(s). This has the effect of limiting the number of competitive legislative districts and leads to an attitude of "Why vote since the outcome is not in doubt?" among many voters.

Still another set of significant deterrents to voter turnout are inconvenient balloting places and short polling times on a work day, as opposed to many European nations which allow voting over a whole weekend. Mexico and Estonia, for example, allow online voting. Similarly, many so-called "voter suppression laws" has been enacted by gerrymandered state legislatures with lopsided majorities of one party (relative to the voter population) that seek to solidify their majority by making it less and less convenient to vote in the hopes discouraging members of the opposing political party from voting. Presumably, these have been enacted in hopes that the many ethnic and economic groups who traditionally vote for the other party will be discouraged by the inconveniences and roadblocks, thereby favoring the current state legislative majorities.

To be fair, single party-dominated legislatures have used the same tactics historically, but in recent times, the Republicans dominate many legislatures and are in a position to pursue this practice. There has been some pushback, however. There was such a hue and cry raised over the results of practices and laws enacted in Florida in 2011 that shortened the time allotted to early voting that even the original cheerleader of these laws, Florida's Governor Rick Scott, recently reversed his position on them.

Disengagement Has Consequences

The consequences of few of those eligible to vote actually voting are significant because they both intended and unintended consequences which affect the performance of American politics and government. Some of the major consequences include:

- ▶ **Increased ideological polarization.** With fewer people voting, the impact of those who do vote is magnified, especially in gerrymandered non-competitive districts where the primary election is often far more important and hard fought than the general election. There is considerable evidence that voters who vote in primaries tend to be wealthier and more ideological than the general electorate and, for that reason, do not represent an accurate cross-section of public opinion. This often leads to the campaigns that target ideological voters and to the election of candidates who represent the more ideological position of the dwindling number of party activists who still vote.

- ▶ **Legislative gridlock.** Because a polarized and diminished electorate results in the election of ideologically-motivated candidates who tend to be at the extremes of the normal political party spectrum, legislative gridlock has become common. Legislators who are true believers in a position are less likely to compromise.

- ▶ **Legislation for the few.** Office-holders tend to reflect the policy and social biases of the above-average-wealth and social-warrior elites who do vote because they know that this group controls the outcome of elections. The disproportionate prevalence of economic elites with an ideological orientation leads to a legislative environment that makes it difficult to enact social programs that favor the many and anger the electorate.

- ▶ **Participation diminishment spiral.** Small and ideologically-driven electorates touch off a vicious cycle by discouraging participation of voters in the middle of the ideological spectrum because they cannot find candidates who represent them.

- ▶ **Negative campaign advertisements.** Negative campaigning and attack ads work in a low-turnout, high-ideology environment because the middle-of-the-road electorate that is repulsed by such campaigning can be ignored by campaign strategists who know they are less likely to vote. As a result, strategists target voter-turnout efforts and sharply-negative campaign commercials toward the ideologically-convincible likely voters who are more likely to accept demonization of those who have sharply different positions.

▶ **Encouragement of special interests.** Interest groups and non-candidate affiliated groups such as the U.S. Chamber of Commerce or Americans for Prosperity are drawn toward such elections and spend lavishly to elect candidates who will support their positions.

▶ **Escalation of campaign costs.** Campaign costs per vote cast continue to rise since entire media markets must be bought for saturation advertising despite a diminishing number of voters among the population reached.

▶ **Easier public opinion manipulation.** Modern information technology and campaign tactics make it relatively easy for interest groups to identify and target the diminished number of likely voters in order to sway public opinion on controversial issues. Direct mail and phone calling with an ideological message are frequently used tools for this, although television remains a potent weapon in this battle.

▶ **Diminution of political parties.** The strong association of religious, economic and single-issue groups with the small number of likely voters weakens the power of political parties while strengthening the power of interest groups.

Chapter Eight

Gridlock In Washington and the States: Causes and Consequences

Government paralysis has become the new normal in Washington, D.C., and in quite a few of the states. The 21st century gridlock, the inability of Congress to pass legislation because of ideological polarization and intense partisanship is part of the problem. So is the seemingly-unending conflict between the Congress and the White House. It is not an exaggeration to say that government has become so effectively dysfunctional that it is unable to respond effectively to the major problems and prospects facing the nation.

Every item on the public agenda becomes an epic ideological battle fought not only within party caucuses but in the media and in the battle for political contributions. This leads to a reluctance, if not an outright refusal, to compromise between the warring factions. Since nobody has a working majority within the separation of powers system, minorities have the ability to block the legislative path desired by majorities. The result is paralysis that slows down government and sometimes actually grinds it to a halt and forces it to shut down.

Items as diverse as formerly-routine debt ceiling extensions, drafting budgets, background checks for gun owners, passage of what used to be a routine transportation bills, and investigations of who was responsible for the attack on the U.S. embassy in Libya lead to partisan wrangling and the inability to act despite an urgent need for governmental action.

While partisanship and ideological bickering in government are nothing new, they have worsened dramatically in the last decade. The cost of such inaction continues to mount.

In the United States, the inability of government to act in the face of pressing needs is beginning to have serious and long-term consequences. We are left with deteriorating infrastructure, government shutdowns, erosion of the legitimacy of government in the eyes of the public, and many similar crises that are unnecessary. All of these negative consequences are primarily driven by this polarization which takes place and is exacerbated by the permissive environment of separation of powers and checks and balances. In more majoritarian democratic systems, such crises lead to a vote of no confidence and new elections and a renewal of the government's mandate rather than gridlock.

The new rage is to say that the government is the cause of all our problems, and if only we had no government, we'd have no problems. I can tell you, that contradicts evidence, history, and common sense.

—William J. Clinton

What causes gridlock?

The major driver of government gridlock in the United States is structural: the exaggerated importance of minorities relative to their share of power. Because the founding fathers distrusted government power so much, even as they created the government, they hamstrung it by building a very complicated system of separation of powers and checks and balances. That makes it very easy for a determined minority with control of any important component of the whole (such as 41 members of the Senate under the modern rule which requires 60% to pass most bills) to use it to their advantage. According to Burt Neuborne, professor at NYU School of Law, in an essay titled *Senate 60-Vote Rule Is An Abuse Of Democracy* writing in *The Hill's* Congressional Blog on April 24, 2013, pens, "But it gets even worse. Since the Constitution requires that each state, regardless of population, be awarded two senators, California's 37 million residents get the same Senate representation as Wyoming's 568,000 hardy souls. Thus, a voter in Wyoming casts a vote for senator that is more than 50 times as powerful as an identical voter in California. 51 senators from 26 states with about 20 percent of the nation's population can constitute a Senate majority.

That is not even all of it. Since the Senate operates under a self-imposed filibuster rule requiring 60 votes to act (except in the case of confirmation of Presidential appointments which now require a simple majority because the Democrats invoked the so-called "nuclear option" when they changed the rules in 2014), Senators representing just 11 percent of the national population can veto laws supported by senators representing 89 percent of the population. That's close to what happened when the Senate voted 55-45 to approve background checks for gun ownership, only to see the legislation fail because it did not reach the artificial 60-vote threshold. When you deconstruct the votes, 46 Senators representing about 65 million

Americans blocked crucial legislation approved by 54 Senators representing about 250 million Americans.

We will not try to replace our founding principles, we will reapply our founding principles.

—Paul Ryan, U.S. Senator

That's not democracy. It's more like being governed by the British House of Lords. It shows the tremendous power of an interest group, in this case, the National Rifle Association, to harness the power of a minority to prevent legislation they like from moving forward despite its popularity."

Short of amending the Constitution's grant of two Senators per state, there isn't much that can be done about giving the residents of California and Wyoming equal representation in the Senate. But the Senate's self-imposed 60-vote requirement is another story. Self-imposed voting rules that render the already mal-apportioned Senate even less democratic violate the "one-Senator one-vote rule" of the 17th Amendment. The "nuclear option" was a step in the right direction but only dealt with a small part of the problem since ordinary legislation still is covered by the 60- vote rule to cut off debate.

That level of malapportionment of representation is not conducive to democracy and contributes to gridlock.

Another set of related factors that drives gridlock is the simultaneous ascendance of ideology and the devaluation of legislative compromise. Because of the widespread practice of gerrymandering perfected by using computer databases to draw legislative district boundaries to favor electing candidates who support those already in power, there are many more "safe" districts than we used to have in Congress. In such districts, the incumbent is almost guaranteed election again and again as long as he or she does not violate the ruling ideology of the district. In other words, what most national and state incumbents fear is not defeat by the opposite party, but having to face a primary opponent put up and funded by powerful interest groups who support a more ideologically "pure" candidate. The primary election defeat of Majority Whip Eric Cantor in 2014 only heightened this fear among members, driving them even more toward ideological fear and into the clutches of well-organized groups at the extremes of American public opinion.

This is seriously exacerbated by the fragmentation of the media. With so many highly opinionated news and opinion sources online and on air, there is less and less audience for the dwindling few national media outlets who have a tradition of balanced coverage, speak approvingly of compromise, accommodation, and, in the process, create common ideas and values of bi-partisanship.

This has led to a steady disintegration of political parties as leavening and broadly mobilizing agents. They have morphed into ideologically-driven coalitions of highly-aggressive interest groups who care about electoral success only to the extent that it supports their cherished causes. Accommodation and compromise are viewed as reprehensible because they dilute progress toward an ideological goal.

Consequences of gridlock.

Gridlock is not merely frustrating. It comes at a high cost. As English political philosopher Edmund Burke observed, "The only thing necessary for the triumph of evil is for good men to do nothing." When governments cannot act to solve national and regional problems, when it cannot seize opportunities to correct evils and create beneficial change, those who profit from the status quo win and the public loses.

In an environment of gridlock, roads crumble because highway funding bills languish, the public interest gets ignored, budgets get arbitrarily sequestered and the nation's (and the states') problems continue to build up with governmental neglect. In other words, hyper-partisanship controls the flow of unwanted legislation by preventing almost all legislation, including good legislation and needed legislation.

The political participation by a broad cross-section of citizens that is so necessary for a functioning democracy also suffers as a result of gridlock. Elections results that are largely predetermined and campaigns that are characterized by extreme ideological positions and negative advertising take their toll on voter turnout.

The existence of a highly-charged ideological atmosphere and a climate that discourages bi-partisanship and compromise also weakens political parties. It makes it far more difficult for political parties to attract good candidates for public office because of the filter of ideological purity. Those who feel the way to pursue the public interest lies in cooperation and give-and-take are less inclined to want to serve in a polarized environment.

Another unfortunate consequence of ideologically-driven gridlock is the decline of policy as a desirable goal and outcome. Yesterday's "policy wonks," those who study or develop strategies and policies with a keen eye on technical details, are fast becoming superseded by ideologues. Fewer legislators concentrate on policy for its own sake and more rely on staffs more than ever before, especially in the environment of term limits. Those staffs, in turn, rely on ideologically-driven interest groups for their policy recommendations and, critically, campaign money. What is lost is the emphasis on good policy.

Chapter Nine

Foreign Policy

The Hubris of Volunteering as International Super Cop

The foreign policy of the United States has been complicated and not entirely successful in the last generation. It has also been frustrating to those who believe that we are the good guys, and that our intervention in other political systems to liberate them and thereby bring them the freedom of our political system is the moral and prudent thing to do. It has not worked out quite that way in the last generation, especially in the Middle East. On the contrary, we found ourselves bogged down in long, costly, and brutal wars of attrition where the lines between the good guys and the bad guys were blurred.

As a superpower with global diplomatic and military reach, a reputation for supporting our allies, and a massive ability to quickly project our forces into virtually any point on the globe, we have been tempted far too often to become involved in civil wars in other lands where the contending sides were ambiguous. As we used our forces to secure our aims, we often found ourselves becoming targets because we were allied with unpopular and often untrustworthy factions and pseudo-tribal groupings in the immensely convoluted politics and theology of the Middle East, northern Africa, and elsewhere.

Once we were involved militarily, we too-often found ourselves bogged down, without a workable plan to extricate ourselves from these conflicts with anywhere near the intended results envisioned when we went into such places as Iraq and Afghanistan. The rapid and successful incursion of I.S. I. S. invaders into Iraq in the aftermath of the U.S. withdrawal of forces is the latest example as of this writing. The U.S. invasion of Iraq, the overthrow of its government, the American occupation and the intensive training of Iraqi armed forces for self-defense seem not to have accomplished much to blunt the reigniting of long-simmering ethnic, religious, and economic conflict. What is more, it has created as many enemies for the United States as friends.

Nor has our influence, foreign and military aid been terribly successful in turning the "Arab Spring" democracy movements into stable and friendly regimes, or ending the brutal civil war in Syria.

Causes

The causes of our foreign policy entanglements are not simple. While some accuse of us of oil imperialism and assume we intervene in places to protect our economic interests, the evidence does not support that as a principal motivating factor of our foreign policy. Yes, we have economic interests and take steps to protect them, but equally significant is that we are also motivated by altruistic interests and a desire to help people. For example, the USA contributed to the rebuilding of post-World War II Europe with the Marshall Plan. The attack on the New York World Trade Center in September 2001 also led us into Afghanistan not on search of new empires but out of a desire to search and destroy of those who attacked us in our homeland.

Based on these observations, I conclude that the desire for military dominance for its own sake or imperialism does not play a decisive role in our foreign policy.

So what causes our foreign policy malaise? One causative factor is our inefficient constitutional system. Our decentralized and inefficient political system makes it possible, even easy, for the President to commit the nation to enter wars without Congressional approval or funding, and hard to extricate ourselves from them once we get in.

Since Congress and the Presidency are not institutionally driven to cooperate, the executive branch often finds it prudent to simply act in the face of a perceived emergency without explicit Congressional authority which may be difficult to obtain in a timely fashion, if at all. Once we are committed, patriotism and the desire to support our troops takes over and the executive branch seeks budgetary and policy authorization from the Congress by presenting the legislators with a fait accompli and warning of being perceived as cowardly if we "cut and run."

War builds a lot of momentum quickly. Once we are entangled, popular displeasure with our foreign policy activities and the Congressional displeasure it stimulates is not an effective path to ending the war since hawks in our separation of powers system can use its leverage on the policy process to prevent withdrawal or defunding action despite their minority status. The anti-war movement engendered by our Viet Nam involvement took years to affect our foreign policy decisively. Moreover, anti-war movements often build countervailing "support our troops" movements that limit their effectiveness. Foreign policy, even in democracies, is not very democratic because, by definition, it is run by technocrats and elites due to the secrecy involved and the complexities of intelligence gathering and strategic decision-making. And in a pseudo-democratic system like the United States, the problem is simply magnified.

The partisanship and gridlock of U.S. politics also enters into the equation. Foreign policy failures such as the attack on the U.S. Consulate in Benghazi, Libya, for example, led to partisan accusations and highly-charged Congressional hearings designed more to embarrass the administration rather than to find facts or to change policies.

From the Army-McCarthy hearings in the beginnings of the cold war to the present, using Congressional hearings and "fact-finding" missions has been a common tactic for those who want to politicize foreign policy despite a cultural norm that foreign policy should be bi-partisan, e.g., the often heard but not-always honored dictum that U.S. politics stops at the water's edge.

Another possible causative factor in our many foreign policy disappointments is our misplaced belief in American exceptionalism. We truly believe that the U.S.A. is unique as a nation and our values and institutions are what the rest of the world needs. It seldom occurs to us when we are contemplating the "saving" of another nation that those we "liberate" do not want and appreciate our political system more than their own and wish to adopt American institutions and practices.

So, our overwhelming military capabilities notwithstanding, the United States of America increasingly appears to be "caught in the chain gang of international relations," as Harvard political scientist Stanley Hoffman described in his influential 1968 book, *Gulliver's Troubles; Or, the Setting of American Foreign Policy* (New York, McGraw-Hill).

After World War II, the United States and the Soviet Union emerged with their power largely intact. Both became world superpowers, armed with nuclear weapons and unchallenged by anybody except each other. This led both nations to fight a long and expensive cold war and to be dragged into often-lethal surrogate conflicts such as Viet Nam to check the perceived global aggressions of our adversaries. When we finally outspent the Soviet Union and emerged victorious from the cold war, we felt very powerful and almost invincible as the surviving superpower.

Unfortunately, our cold war victory was somewhat hollow and short-lived. We were neither as invincible as we thought due to the huge debt we undertook to win the cold war, the massive costs we continue to incur to maintain dominance, our thirst for foreign-produced energy, the rise of global terrorism, and the ability of smaller powers to be very painful thorns in our side and even to attack our homeland. The bi-polar post-war world with two major powers became, in very short order, a brief mono-polar world where the U.S. was the only superpower and acted accordingly by intervening in Somalia, Eastern Europe, and invading Iraq, for example.

However, just as we started to get used to and plan how to exploit our alleged dominance as the world's only superpower, another superpower was slowly emerging to challenge our interests worldwide. Other regional powers and terrorist groups with capabilities of mass-destruction weaponry have emerged to create a confusing international system that has elements of both bi-polarity and multi-polarity simultaneously. Such an international system is both complex and potentially unstable. As a result, the frustrations of U. S. foreign policy continue unabated.

Domestic policy can only defeat us; foreign policy can kill us.

—John F. Kennedy

Consequences of U.S. Foreign Policy

The consequences of our beliefs in the moral underpinnings of our policies, our so-called military invincibility, and the exaggeration of our influence are significant. It has led directly to the hubris of believing that we could influence political outcomes and change regimes in Asia and the Middle East. Both of these areas have long-standing cultures that have far different histories and cultures from the U.S.A. They have coalitions and conflicts between them that have their roots in hundreds of years of history. To put it mildly, our interventions in these areas did not work out well and we had little clue as to what the players really wanted and what we were getting ourselves into.

Whether we were motivated by altruism, national interest, economic gain, or a combination of them, we entered into these troubled areas with no clear goals. Consequently, we had a very difficult time articulating our goals and aims for intervention except for vague notions of projecting freedom and democracy with even vaguer goals of protecting American interests by establishing allies, influence, and bases in volatile parts of the globe.

One result is that we have overextended ourselves dangerously by fighting wars on several fronts simultaneously. We have overworked our military resources so that many of the best units in our volunteer forces have become fatigued with deployment after deployment. In short, we got ourselves bogged down in long wars of attrition that caused us to take (and exact) horrendous casualties. We are spending ourselves so deeply into debt that future generations will have to continue to pay tremendous opportunity costs for our choices. Instead of having money to renew our crumbling domestic infrastructure, modernize our outdated transportation system, and improve a health system that is extremely costly and produces outcomes that lag far behind other industrialized nations, our heirs will be faced with having to pay for our wars for generations to come.

Another likely consequence of our attempts at being the world's policeman is that we have curtailed our own freedoms far more than would have been required if we were not involved in Middle Eastern wars. Our exposure overseas, combined with fear and outrage about the wanton attack on September 11, 2001, led us to enact overly-draconian legislation such as The Patriot Act and curtail freedoms and spy on our own citizens in order to provide a sense of security. In the process, we have inched closer to becoming a garrison state because of our preoccupation with security and foreign influence that far exceeds the sensible goal of maintaining a deterrence against aggression by those who do not like us. A nation cannot be on a war footing for decades without domestic consequences.

All of this might be worth it if we were fighting for our lives as we were in World War II, or actually succeeding in advancing clear and worthwhile foreign policy goals. But despite the tremendous costs we have paid for our foreign policy in the last generation, we have neither succeeded in establishing free and democratic regimes elsewhere nor in creating a pro-American attitude, nor a continuing welcome for our presence among the populations of the areas we have fought in and for. Nor have we received any major domestic payoffs for our overseas interventions.

On the contrary, rather than accomplishing our aims, the conflicts in which we have intervened and hoped to settle still exist. The fighting that pre-existed our intervention quickly resumes in many places upon our exit. What we have succeeded at is creating a resentment of our policies and culture in large sectors of these foreign lands because of our presence and the collateral damage that our military activities produced in those societies. This resentment has led to the United States being blamed for conflicts that long pre-dated our involvement, and has put a target on our backs and makes America a tempting target for terrorists who are looking for a scapegoat for their own policy failures. The necessary actions we take to prosecute a war in a foreign land become potent recruiting tools for our enemies.

Another alarming consequence of the hubris of our foreign policy is that by weakening ourselves by fighting long, costly, and ultimately futile wars, we hasten the inevitable rise of rival powers such as China and Al Qaeda.

Chapter Ten

Dueling Economic Approaches

The Disintegration of the New Deal and the Fraying Safety Net

As the great depression deepened its stranglehold on the U.S. and world economies in the 1930's, it became painfully obvious to many economists and policy makers that the "invisible hand" market system of classical economic theory did not always work for the public benefit. Even though private enterprise provided periods of prosperity for some, it also produced periods of bust between booms and even the booms were not beneficial to all. This left a large, seemingly permanent underclass who faced chronic unemployment, underemployment, and even the threat of starvation.

The severity of the great depression was alarming to many economic thinkers and policy makers. They perceived it as far more serious than a downturn taking place in the normal boom-and-bust economic cycle. They feared that we were tottering on an economic abyss and that the great depression could transition into permanent depression unless something drastic was done.

One thinker in particular, influential British economist John Maynard Keynes, wrote in his book, *The General Theory of Employment, Interest and Money*, published in 1936, that the way to save the market system was for governments to intervene to smooth out the business cycle and cushion its excesses. He and his advocates maintained that in the short run, especially during recessions, government investment in the economy was needed to shore up society and that it should be paid for by surpluses accumulated during good times. It was supported by influential American economists and political thinkers of the era and was the policy pursued by the Roosevelt Administration.

Because it worked in practice to mitigate the Great Depression and put people back to work, Keynesian economics emerged as the most widely-accepted economic paradigm in Western developed nations during the late 1930's. The U.S. government invested heavily (despite initial Supreme Court opposition) in economic development programs such as the Works Progress Administration and social programs like Social Security. Government spending was accelerated even more as World

War II threatened and continued largely unabated into the post-war economic expansion. The period of 1945–1973 saw high levels of U. S. government spending in domestic infrastructure such as the creation of Interstate Highway and Defense program, and social programs such as farm subsidies and housing assistance and high military spending. It was also an era of relative prosperity for the U.S. although there were ups and downs. A safety net for the disadvantaged was built and a strong middle class emerged. The part of Keynesian economic theory that called for paying for intervention with surpluses in good times was not followed, however, and an era of huge and seemingly-permanent government deficits emerged and continues to the present. Economists are still hotly debating the significance and consequences of large deficits and, despite the certainty of the Tea Party and fiscal ultra-conservatives in the U.S., the issues of whether deficits are harmful and, if so, at what level and for what length of time, are far from settled.

> *The end of democracy and the defeat of the American Revolution will occur when government falls into the hands of lending institutions and moneyed incorporations.*

> —Thomas Jefferson, 1816

Keynesian economics as it played out in the U.S. advocates a mixed economy—predominantly led by the private sector, but accommodating a fairly significant government intervention during recessions and the continuing support of social programs that encouraged and subsidized the growth of a strong middle class. In Europe, there was even more emphasis on social programs and a more faith in government programs.

While Keynesianism became associated with ruling liberal governments in Europe and the preferred economic path between the 1930's and the 1970's in the U.S., it was not the only game in town. From the beginning, it was opposed by the libertarians and supporters of Milton Friedman and the Chicago School of classical economists. Although not then in the majority, they continued to attack Keynesianism. A growing minority agreed and advocated a change back to laissez faire and small government. The downward economic cycle touched off by the rise of the Arab oil cartel and the resulting stagflation of the 1970's led to further erosion of the prevailing Keynesian paradigm.

Libertarians and their latest manifestation, the Tea Party movement, (backed by enormously wealthy and politically active business interests like the Koch brothers) continued and escalated a relentless campaign to win the "hearts and minds" war of the U.S. public and the governing elites. They scored a resounding victory with the election of Ronald Reagan as President. He adopted anti-government rhetoric although his anti-government policies were far more nuanced than those of the present anti-government movement.

Today, the anti-Keynesian movement has largely succeeded in undermining faith in the basic methodology and assumptions of Keynesian economics and popular support for government as an instrument of civic betterment in the U.S. Gradually, the right wing of the Republican Party elected sympathetic governors, majorities in state legislatures (who perpetuated their rule through gerrymandering), Presidents Ronald Reagan (who was more conservative in rhetoric than economic policy) and George W. Bush, and a majority on the supreme court which became more pro-business and anti-government. The anti-Keynesians succeeded in capturing the Republican Party and now have a headlock on Congress with their control of the House of Representatives. They have effectively held the rest of the government hostage by proclaiming that they will support no legislation that does not meet their budgetary criteria of being fiscally neutral.

Keynesian economics is now effectively dormant, if not dead. The cost has been significant to the middle class and to confidence in the social safety net that has been in place since the 1930's. Kathryn Tuggle's *What's Happening to the Middle Class?*, published August 23, 2012, by FOXBusiness.com, wrote, "America's middle class has just endured one of the worst decades in modern history, according to a new study by the Pew Research Center. In the last 10 years, members of the middle class have watched their wages decrease along with their net worth, and have reported an overall more difficult time making ends meet."

According to the study, "The Lost Decade of the Middle Class," 85% of middle class Americans say it is "more difficult now than it was a decade ago... to maintain their standard of living." The middle class is also a dwindling population: Today only 51% of Americans fall into the middle class, down from 61% in 1971. Interestingly, it seemed that economic mobility moved in two directions because it has turned out that some members of the middle class are upwardly mobile as the percentage of wealthy families rose from 14% to 20%, while those falling into lower income categories rose to 29% from 25%.

In just one year [2011 figures], members of the middle class have seen their median household income fall to $69,487 from $72,956 in 2010. Over the last 10 years, household net worth has also dropped dramatically— down to $93,150 from $129,582 in 2001."

While the laissez-faire economists attribute these trends to too much government, public opinion (as analyzed in the Pew Data) attributes the problems to elite selfishness. "62% say 'a lot' of the blame for the struggles lies with Congress, while 54% fault banks and financial institutions and 47% point to 'large corporations.' Other things blamed included the Bush administration, the Obama administration, and foreign competition...8% say they will never recover from the damage done during the Great Recession. And 26% say their children's standard of living will be worse than their own."

The U.S. political right has vigorously opposed even the little social legislation that has passed recently. The GOP-led House has voted to repeal the Affordable Care Act of 2010 over 80 times and shows no sign of giving up, continuing to bash it in 2014 mid-term election television commercials. They are fierce opponents of tighter banking regulation and generally opposed the bail-out of G.M. and Chrysler. Despite the fact that limited government intervention imposed by the outgoing Bush administration and advanced in the Obama Presidency did work (rescuing General Motors and saving the banking system again, for example). It has changed neither their minds nor their campaign for public opinion. The libertarians have won the war for our hearts and minds, facts notwithstanding.

While U.S. social service spending (mostly on health care) has continued to rise even during the "Great Recession" of the last several years, it has not risen nearly as fast as Keynesians advocate since they believe that aggressive government spending is needed during recessions and the national debt can be reduced later, in times of prosperity. Most Keynesians also believe that the amount of U.S. debt is sustainable at present levels of gross national product and that the recovery from the Great Recession would have been far more robust with more government spending.

Europe, too, is moving to trim its welfare state in the 21st century due to overextension and budget excesses, but even after cuts, European government spending is still at a much higher level than the U.S. According to the Heritage Foundation, government spending in 2012 as a percentage of GNP was 38.9% in the U.S. but 43.7% in Germany, 50% in Belgium and 47.3% in the U.K. and 39.7% in Canada.

Stemming the rise of government spending (particularly social spending) and cutting budgets are the oft-stated priorities of the U.S. right. Driven by ideological distrust of government and a faith in the social utility of the "invisible hand," they continue to vote against federal spending and to advocate cutbacks of federal programs, transfer of many programs to the states, and smaller government in general. If they prevail, more programs like the across-the-board spending cuts enacted in 2013 (the "sequester") will become the norm despite the ability of the well-connected to save most of their cherished programs, e.g., farm subsidies, defense spending, oil industry subsidies, and subsidies for airlines and truckers through federal expenditures on the airways system and highways, etc.

If the anti-Keynesians continue their success, it is likely that the U.S. will begin to actually dismantle the safety net that the Keynesians erected and that has led to the growth and prosperity of the American middle class. Programs like food assistance, infrastructure renewal, Amtrak, and government health care assistance would face a dismal future in spite of widespread support for them and a demonstrable need. The survival of a robust U.S. middle class would be in jeopardy.

PART III: Moving The Political System of The United States Toward Democracy

"To view the opposition as dangerous is to misunderstand the basic concepts of democracy. To oppress the opposition is to assault the very foundation of democracy."

—Aung San Suu Kyi, *Letters from Burma*

Chapter 11

Summarizing the Malaise of American Democracy

Moving Toward Change

The purposes of the analyses in this book are both analytical and normative. First, we seek to understand and explain our civic and constitutional environment and, in the process, to disassociate our analysis with either jingoistic, blind patriotism that proclaims everything we do to be star-crossed, or the often-expressed pessimism of what remains of the American left that proclaims that we have gone too far away from cherished values like equality and justice and, as a result, it is too late to turn the juggernaut around—so it is futile to embark on a program of civic renewal because the forces of reaction will doom it to failure.

Secondly, as we understand the issues and obstacles we face, our goal is to explore, evaluate and endorse widely proposed (and some not-yet-widely-proposed) improvements, solutions, and reforms to our system with an eye toward civic renewal and increased democratic vitality in our third century. Underlying this is my belief that The United States of America has been, deserves to be, and will continue to be a great nation with a tremendous potential to be a decent place to live and a good citizen of the world.

The author strongly believes that the need for reform and democracy is great and can happen. All is not lost for the U.S.A. despite our problems and how far the forces of reaction and government distrust have progressed. On the contrary, I assume that much can be done to keep the United States on track as one of history's greatest political achievements. If we develop mid-course reforms that insure civic renewal, we will stay on track. If we refuse to be self-critical and insist on staying the course regardless of a changing world, we risk civic derailment and missed opportunities for our citizens.

The Emergence of the Conditions for Democracy

The nation governed by the 21st century U. S. Constitution may have the same name as the nation that the authors of the 1787 constitution were familiar with as they deliberated how to govern themselves, but there are more differences than similarities between the United States of America in 1789, when the constitution took effect, and late 2014, as I write this.

For one thing, the nation is vastly bigger than the founders envisioned it would become as far as they could peer into the future. Now, it stretches across the entire continent and spans 3,717,813 square miles, making it the third largest nation in the world. Despite this growth, in practical democratic terms the nation is far smaller than it was in 1787 since transportation and communications are radically better and that has profound implications for democratic politics. The potential electorate is now able to travel from coast to coast in hours, and journey to neighboring states and towns with ease. There is far more cross-state residential mobility than earlier generations, providing more homogeneity between regions and less of a case for representing states rather than people.

Communications have followed a similar path of massive change. Democracy depends on an electorate with access to information so voters can register intelligent votes. Today, information on public policy and politically-relevant events spreads to the far reaches of the nation in real time in many cases, and is disseminated around the clock through media that range from national newspapers and round-the-clock cable TV networks to Twitter, the Internet, and texting. Government actions and opposition to those acts move through the political system almost instantaneously, through thousands of different filters. By contrast, in 1789, it often took weeks for information to travel via horseback or sailing ship to reach the elites who held the levers of power. The common citizens often never received it until it was moot.

The education and literacy level of the population has increased dramatically as well. Today, a much larger percentage of the population can read and has the background to understand and evaluate information about public policy issues, compared to 1787.

With a population approaching 320 million and is characterized by an ethnic diversity that would have been staggering to the founding generation, the population generates a great deal more issues and need for government than in the 1780's. The economy, too, has grown dramatically bigger and radically more complex over the centuries. This creates a critical need to foster and regulate interstate and international commerce—a major priority as well as a gargantuan task requiring complex regulatory and administrative agencies.

The United States also operates in a far more complex international system with far more at stake. Not only is trade and relationships with other nations at risk, but life and death can literally hang in the balance in a nuclear and bio-warfare era.

Together, these changes have made the United States a fertile ground for increased democracy to take root. Given the magnitude and the direction of this evolution, it is not surprising that so many challenges to the constitutional order have developed. Even though the constitution is constantly changing, the magnitude and directions of the changes (not all of them reforms) in the original constitution that have evolved to date are neither adequate to the task nor very democratic. Whether democracy was either possible or advisable with the electorate of 1787, it is certainly possible now, and, as the central theme of this book suggests, it is advisable as well.

I've always tried to explain democracy is not perfect. But it gives you a chance to shape your own destiny.

—Aung San Suu Kyi

Obstacles and Issues

As we turn our attention to changes we should make to accomplish a democratic civic renewal, it is an opportune time to review the obstacles and issues we face.

For analytical purposes, it makes sense to classify these issues as being caused by either policy and cultural choices made within our constitutional framework, or as issues which are fundamentally structural, e.g., are caused by the constitutional environment and are largely independent of policy.

Our political culture (the basic attitudes and civic assumptions which we share and which influence our policies and institutions) is characterized by a pervasive distrust of government that has its roots in our experience as a British colony. It is further perpetuated and encouraged by powerful, well-financed laissez-faire advocates who want the freedom to operate without government regulation or limitation. As we shall examine in subsequent chapters, this costs our political system dearly. We face formidable challenges to developing an effective democratic government within a political culture that neither likes nor trusts government and misperceives democracy so substantially.

American political culture hinders the development of a consistent and cost-effective social safety net such as most of the world relies upon. It also weakens our ability to develop and maintain the critical infrastructure and government programs and regulations needed in a modern large nation. It has also started to limit us economically as our middle class has declined, and with it, the middle class's ability to purchase our goods and services and stoke the fires of our economy. While having an economy that is fair and a solid social safety net is not an absolute prerequisite to democracy, a large middle class that is economically secure has been a bedrock foundation of successful democracies in Europe and elsewhere. Distrust in government in general is corrosive to democracy by definition since democracy is fundamentally a form of government.

We are also saddled with a significant misperception of democracy itself. Since we believe that the American political system is the epitome of democracy perfected, we feel little need to enact reforms that would make our system more democratic. Attempts by reformers to expand the franchise and the reach of general elections on either the national or sub-national level meet with little success in such a policy environment. This has led to many restrictions on who can vote in U.S. history, and an attitude that voting is a privilege to be granted by elites to those who go along rather than a basic human right in a democratic political system.

Democracy properly understood in either its direct or representative iterations is certainly not a perfect form of government, but, as Winston Churchill wisely observed in a previously-mentioned Parliamentary speech on November 11, 1947, "Democracy is the worst form of government, except for all those other forms that have been tried from time to time."

Over the long stretch of history, a convincing claim can be made that while democracies are not immune to the enormous policy mistakes that all political systems make, they make fewer major blunders and correct them faster than other types of political organization.

The other set of issues that our political system faces is intrinsic to our republican constitutional framework. A constitutional framework, as understood by most political scientists, is not simply the words written in a document called the constitution, but the entire constellation of fundamental principles and meanings that form and regulate the institutions, laws, and policies of a political system. Words inscribed in a document must inevitably be interpreted since circumstances change and cannot be anticipated completely.

For example, the concept and practical meaning of *privacy* in an age of widespread intercepts of communication by government and the existence of unmanned drones with both intelligence-gathering and offensive capabilities was not (and could not have been) anticipated by the constitution writers of the 1780's, and is being constitutionally interpreted today on an almost daily basis and at a variety of judicial and political levels. So too is the interstate commerce clause of the constitution as it applies to the rights and responsibilities of the federal government, the states and local governments to build, maintain and regulate roads, the national airways system, public commercial waterways, and a national rail passenger system.

Who interprets and has the final say in such issues is so important that it constitutes a major defining factor among political systems. Democracies tend to favor either the population or its elected representatives as designated constitutional interpreters and republics and oligarchies tend to place constitutional interpretation powers in the hands of a small group such as a council of judges or an oligarchy or even a monarch or dictator. In the U.S. we leave that to the appointed-for-life Supreme Court and lower courts while, for example, parliamentary systems usually charge the legislature with that task.

As a separation of powers republic with partial rather than general elections (albeit with some democratic institutions such as the U.S. House of Representatives), the U.S. political system is quite resistant to populous-driven constitutional change and tends to perpetuate groups in power once they have achieved it. Since all branches must be coordinated for major constitutional change to take place, it usually does not or lags far behind the need.

In essence, the contemporary political culture of the United States provides a climate that is hostile to reform and significant constitutional change despite the fact that the more than 80,000 collective governments of the United States are experiencing an escalating and serious mismatch between what they need to do in the 21st century to "maintain a more perfect union and provide for the common defense." While few would dispute that the nation is more complex and crowded than it was in 1789, many would and do resist substantial changes to the body of U.S. law, tradition, political culture, and constitutional structures that still reflect the anti-democratic goals and practices of the founders. Change has happened but has not kept pace with the need for political institutions to adapt and deal with changing conditions and a more democratically-capable citizenry.

This is the perfect civic storm that we have discussed so far. We are facing government gridlock, low voter turnout and engagement, special interest dominance, and a declining national infrastructure. We are also experiencing an increasingly incoherent and inconsistent foreign policy and social programs that cost too much and perform poorly. None of these bode well for our future unless we can change. Fortunately, knowledge is power and we can change and become a more democratic and responsive nation if we agree that we have problems and unite at least in broad terms on some things we can and should do, e.g., increasing our democratic institutions and practices to make things better.

Chapter Twelve

A Modest Catalogue of Democratic Reforms

As preceding chapters have suggested and the evidence of all-too-familiar headlines about government conflict and ineffectiveness reinforce, the political system of the United States of America is becoming increasingly dysfunctional. The October, 2013 government shutdown precipitated by Tea Party sympathizers in Congress who demanded defunding of the Affordable Care Act before they would vote for a temporary budget extension is only the latest in a continuing series of confrontations and failures to govern. All of this takes place in the environment of structural characteristics of the system that can be exploited for partisan purposes. This frequently is a ploy of ideological zealots.

Increasing the limits of the national debt, passage of Congressional budgets, ratification of judicial and other appointments and extensions of highway funding bills used to be routine. Now, they are the subjects of partisan deadlock and such conflict is the rule rather than the exception.

Can anything be done about this dysfunction? Has the increasingly complex world finally overwhelmed our 18th century political system and pushed it over the brink of slow decline toward the rocks of gridlock below?

As the title of this book suggests, perhaps fueled by a combination of hopeful optimism and ample historical evidence, political systems can reform themselves and are thusly "fixable." I believe that something—a lot—can be done to catalyze democratic civic renewal and modern governance to our political system in the 21st century. Increasing the level of democracy in our political system (and thereby creating an incentive for the government to be more responsive to majorities) would take the United States a long way down the path of civic reform.

To begin our journey toward prescription, a useful approach is to categorize the democratic reforms needed into proximate versus long-range constitutional solutions.

The proximate solutions are more policy-oriented than constitutional. They are attractive because they can be accomplished in a relatively short period of time once a consensus emerges. They do not require major constitutional amendments that would fundamentally alter the nature of our separation of powers system. Also, since policy inevitably impacts constitutional evolution over the long run, they are good precursors to the more fundamental constitutional change that might be needed to nudge the system closer to democracy.

Longer-range and more substantial constitutional solutions would have far more impact than these proximate solutions. These would cause a substantial change in our basic constitutional framework rather than constitutional tinkering to transform it into a representative democracy. For this reason, they are less likely to happen since that would require the development of a consistently larger consensus over a very long period of time.

To succeed, those of us who see the need for reform would be well-served to start "small" and "merely" make substantial changes to some of our policies and procedures, keeping in mind our long-range objective of bringing democratic civic renewal to our political system.

Proximate Reforms

Turning our attention to the proximate solutions, it is important to observe that at best, any real change and reform of a political system as large, well-established, and complex as that of the United States, will neither come quickly nor easily. It is far from assured that a consensus can be built to catalyze even these modest reforms. Nevertheless, it is certainly worth the effort to work toward developing awareness and agreement on these solutions.

By way of full disclosure, the fundamental rationale driving the following catalogue of proximate reforms is the same motivation that will drive the prescriptions for long-range reform that will be detailed later in this book: increasing the amount of democracy in the U.S. political system.

The rationale is simple but very difficult to refute: Churchill was correct when he said in 1947 that "democracy is the worst form of Government except all those other forms that have been tried from time to time."

Pushing hard against the twin inertial forces of the widespread belief that our political system is already democratic, and the misunderstanding of the damage done to our system by separation of powers, I offer these reforms as an incomplete but still meaningful catalogue of things that need to be done to fix some of the pressing problems within our political system and move us toward a democratic civic renewal. As a caveat, even though they are proximate and accomplishable in principle, the task of accomplishing them should not be underestimated.

Given the present state of American political culture, even these relatively modest reforms will be very controversial. Reforms that will depend on a consensus for change that has yet to emerge. Their virtue is that they are indeed proximate. As controversial and difficult as they are to accomplish, they are still less controversial and probably need less support (perhaps a smaller majority) to get them enacted as compared to the long-range solutions.

> *The Voting Rights Act of 1965 was indeed a vital instrument of democracy, ensuring the integrity and reliability of a democratic process that we as a Country hold so dear.*

> —Charles B. Rangel (U.S. Congressman)

Job Number One: Increasing the Effectiveness, Fairness and Impact of Elections

Currently, elections in the United States are run by the 50 states. This gives the legislative majorities in each state significant leeway to shape its own rules and districts.

In the wake of the recent Supreme Court decision (Shelby County v. Holder) which gutted much of the 1965 Voting Rights Act by holding the requirement that states with a history of voting discrimination get preclearance before changing voting rules to be unconstitutional, states can (and do) make their own election rules, and can make it difficult for voters to register and vote. The so-called "voter suppression acts" by Republican-dominated legislatures that created obstacles to easy registration and convenient voting belong in this category. These obstacles need to be abolished. A set of national standards for open and convenient elections needs to be legislated by Congress and upheld by the courts.

The issue remains quite controversial. Florida voters, for example, passed a "fair districts" amendment to the state constitution outlawing gerrymandering in 2010. The Republican-dominated legislature (in a state that has a slim majority of Democrats) redistricted Congressional seats in 2012 to continue to favor Republicans. On July 10, 2014, a Florida judge threw out the 2012 congressional redistricting plan and found that Republicans "conspired to manipulate the boundaries to protect the party's majority in Washington and 'made a mockery' of the rules of transparency in the process." He ordered that two districts be redrawn because they violated the standard approved by voters in 2010 to ban legislators from favoring or protecting incumbents. Five days later, Republicans in the Florida legislature announced they would not appeal the ruling but asked for a delay in implementation until 2016. The delay was granted.

In order to satisfy the most fundamental principles of democracy, the U.S. needs to create fairer and more democratic elections by:

▶ Re-establishing the one-person-one-vote standard by outlawing the practice of creating districts that favor one party of incumbent because of the demographic makeup of the district. Violations of this standard should be punishable by severe penalties up to and including removal from office for those found to be usurping this basic right. In its place, we need to create a national non-partisan districting commission made up of representatives from all major political parties including a group of political scientists, geographers, and demographers. They would be mandated to follow the one-person-one-vote principal for all national and state elections and to avoid partisan bias. This commission should be appointed by the President and ratified by Congress.

▶ Instituting binding national referenda on policy issues that can override acts of Congress such as those that routinely take place in Switzerland. Since the referenda would be national, identical language should be on every ballot regardless of jurisdiction. Votes should be counted in a national pool with the majority winning. The Federal Election Commission should be charged with creating standards for clarity of ballot language, criteria for inclusion on the ballot, and for overseeing and counting ballots for these referenda.

▶ Passing a new Voting Rights Act that mandates national election rules that must be followed by every state. Effectively outlawing state control over elections, the act should determine who is eligible to vote, what credentials must be presented to vote, when and how voters should be registered, and how registrations are transferred between jurisdictions.

- ► The act should abolish rules requiring voter registration a month in advance and allow day-of-election registration. This can easily be implemented with modern computers and reasonable security provisions. People who become motivated to vote during a campaign can do so. It should also allow people to cast their ballot any day from Saturday through Tuesday of election week so people with varying family and work schedules can be accommodated. Along the same lines, online voting with appropriate security authentication and safeguards should be adopted. If banks trust us to bank using accounts online, shouldn't governments trust us to vote online too?

- ► Strong steps need to be taken to minimize the role of money in politics. This would level the playing field for those who are not billionaires but want to influence public policy. The minimum component of this would be the repeal of Citizens United vs. Federal Election Commission decision by the Supreme Court that prohibited the government from restricting political spending by independent groups including unions and corporations, thus equating free spending with free speech.

- ► To give this equalization of the campaign playing field real teeth and allow candidates and parties without access to vast sums of wealth to get their message across during election campaigns, we should institute public financing of campaigns (matching small citizen contributions) combined with limits on spending and provision of ample free media time for candidates. This is a common practice in Europe and South America and seems to work well. It is preferable to the current system which encourages "pay to play" political access.

Chapter Thirteen

Political Literacy:
A critical Prerequisite to Viable Democracy

Democratic elections depend on the premise that those who vote have enough information and the ability to process that information in a way that allows them to understand and evaluate the issues involved. Citizens who do not recognize the basic defining characteristics of democracy and whether their nation practices them are hard pressed to understand its pros and cons and to be intelligent voters as well as to support policies and policy makers that promote democracy.

In short, civic literacy is critical to a functioning and sustainable democracy. Toward this end, high on our list of proximate democratic reforms in the contemporary U.S. political system is the fostering and sustaining of an educated citizenry. It is very difficult for democracy to endure in a nation with a population that is civically illiterate and unable to recognize (much less resist) attempts to manipulate them through propaganda and biased information.

Fostering civic literacy has long been a part of U.S. history. A recent Fact Sheet published by the Campaign for the Civic Mission of Schools (www.civicmissionofschools.org) observed that "the founders of our universal system of free public education made education for citizenship a core part of the mission of public education, equal to workplace preparation." They defined the civic mission of schools as the "determination to educate young Americans about their rights and responsibilities as citizens."

For example, Thomas Jefferson wrote in a letter to Richard Price in 1789 that "Whenever the people are well-informed, they can be trusted with their own government." Similarly, he wrote to Charles Yancey in January, 1816 that "If a nation expects to be ignorant and free, in a state of civilization, it expects what never was and never will be."

Over two centuries later, Nigerian author Chinua Achebe remarked in a January 2012 interview with the Christian Science Monitor that, "A functioning, robust democracy requires a healthy educated, participatory followership and an educated, morally-grounded leadership."

Sadly, we do not meet these criteria with consistency. Americans are not terribly literate when it comes to politics and government. As evidence, we cite the results of a scientific survey conducted by the Center for the Study of the American Dream at Xavier University in 2012. The survey found that one third of Americans polled failed to answer six out of ten questions correctly. Fifty percent could not answer seven out of ten questions correctly. How tough were the questions? It is the exact naturalization test that must be passed by those desiring to become U.S. citizens. 97.5% of immigrants passed this test with at least 60% in 2010.

More evidence of the failure of the U.S. to adequately foster civic education has been gathered in a survey of state and district policies. The Education Commission of the States. The National Center for Learning and Citizenship (www.ecs.org) found that, "In recent years, civic learning has been increasingly pushed aside. Until the 1960s, three courses in civics and government were common in American high schools. Two of them ("civics" and "problems of democracy") explored the role of citizens and encouraged students to discuss current issues. Today those courses are very rare. What remains is a course on "American government" that usually spends little time on how people can—and why they should—participate as citizens."

Further, as of 2011, only 19 states include civic learning in their state assessment/accountability systems. Civics is a part of an overall social studies assessment which includes history, geography, state history, and economics. These tests concentrate on factual knowledge that can be measured on a 'true/false, fill in the bubble' test format, rather than determining if the student has knowledge of why and how a citizen should be engaged." (NCLC @ ECS state policies database.)

The recent national emphasis on STEM education (science, technology, engineering and mathematics) is a good thing because it fosters some of the skills needed for the United States to compete internationally and to maintain our economy. But it does little or nothing to empower us democratically and to strengthen the basic civic infrastructure that contributes to our economic and political stability. Such civic literacy would also makes the United States a more desirable international partner and locus for foreign investment. Unfortunately, the national No Child Left Behind Act that dominated U.S. education policy for the last generation put little emphasis on civic education.

A nation with a highly-developed educational system that aspires to be a democracy must do better. The need is important and urgent, given our abominable and dangerous lack of civic literacy. Fortunately, better civic literacy is also accomplishable if we make a serious and sustained national commitment to universal and in-depth civic education. It would not require major constitutional changes, although it is certain to be controversial and anger "states' rights" advocates.

What is needed is a major nationwide upgrading of civic education and lifelong learning about the workings of the U.S. political system in the context of comparative political institutions, major currents of political thought (including a general ability to define liberty, equality, justice and democracy), and fostering of basic analytical skills so citizens can develop a conceptual framework to process and apply the information they have learned.

At a minimum, the components of better civic education for the United States must encompass:

▶ Creation of an objective, non-partisan model curriculum and courseware for universal civic education studies at all K-12 grade levels. It should emphasize comparative political systems, political thought, and democratic citizen participation. It should be created by a blue-ribbon task force composed of political scientists and other relevant subject-matter experts rather than professional pedagogues and school administrators.

▶ Enactment of a national universal civic education mandate for all K-12 schools based on the above curriculum. This should be a federally-funded mandate. Schools that do not comply should be subject to withdrawal of all federal aid and their administrators should be subject to criminal penalties.

▶ Enactment of a national civics teacher certification mandate that requires all teachers of civics be trained extensively in the subject (equivalent to an undergraduate major in the subject).

We can no longer allow those who teach a critical subject like civics to hold a teaching certificate in another subject to be certified on the basis of taking a few educational methods courses. These technique courses provide them with little or no knowledge of government and political science to qualify them to teach this critical subject.

► Since it is a fact of educational life that if a given subject is not tested for, it is not taught, we must create and implement a national civic literacy test based on the model K-12 civic education curriculum by the same task force that designed the curriculum.

► Enactment of a requirement for a 70% passing score on the national civic literacy test as a prerequisite to the awarding of a high school diploma.

► Requirements for at least one basic political science course that is, at a minimum, a college-level version of the model public school civics curriculum. This should be a prerequisite for a degree from any college, university, or accredited institution of higher education including two-year colleges.

► Creation of a free Lifelong Civic Education Academy that operates online and offers occasional seminars in major cities. The Academy will continue civics education for those no longer in school. It should operate simultaneously at a variety of levels to provide both basic and advanced civic knowledge and analytical abilities. It should be administered by a board of directors made up of political scientists and other qualified academics.

To increase its impact, a small tax incentive should be offered to successful "graduates" of the program who can certify that they maintain their continuing civic education, It might also be possible to raise private funds to provide merchandise or other valued incentives for those who participate.

► Requiring via an amendment to the federal Voting Rights Act that all state and local governments publish and effectively disseminate factual information about voting rights and opportunities in their districts.

The quality of democracy and the quality of journalism are deeply entwined.

—Bill Moyers

Better Journalism

Most people not in school and many who are still students get whatever civic information they absorb (both facts and the spin put upon those facts) from the mass media. Thus, better civic education depends as much on good journalism as it does on good civic education.

Unfortunately, the media landscape of the United States does not lend itself to this task very well. With significant exceptions such as public television and public radio, today's media tends to emphasize headlines and scandals. Most often, in-depth analysis and understanding of political affairs and world events is lacking. What analysis that is offered all too frequently is ideological fabrication of facts to support a political agenda rather than an objective analysis and explanation.

This fabrication-masquerading-as-analysis too often the output we get from non-objective, biased media. They produce fantasy stories and interpretations of facts motivated by partisan biases and serve to bait, encourage, and even form the ideological misperceptions of listeners/readers/viewers. The audience is part of this analytical charade and encourages it by their very existence because they listen to, watch, or read those media that reinforce their personal biases and make them feel good, and thus produce high ratings for such shows. Many major news media (especially some TV networks and syndicated radio talk shows) have essentially abandoned neutrality and traditional standards of journalistic objectivity and actively pursue an ideological agenda. Even those who still strive for objective reporting have seen cutbacks in news budgets, and many offer less reporting and thoughtful commentary than in the past.

Since freedom of speech and the press are such fundamental prerequisites to democracy, I do not advocate governmental mandating of what the media must cover, or an imposition of intellectual standards upon them. No matter how this might improve the quality of journalism in the short run, its long-term consequences could be disastrous for democracy because of the potential chilling effect it could have on dissenters and loyal opponents of the government.

Instead, I advocate more support for the competition—the media who emphasize in-depth analysis and objective reporting. While they are far from perfect, National Public Radio and The Public Broadcasting Service (PBS) do a better job of covering government and politics than the commercial TV and radio networks. These services should be well-funded to continue to do so. If they have sufficient funds to do their job and expand their offerings, and if they are insulated via long-range funding from the pressures of those in power at any given time, they can continue to serve as beacons of good practice and, in the process, perhaps stir the commercial networks to do better.

Chapter Fourteen

Restoring Majority Rule in Congress

The 113th Congress, elected in 2012 (with two thirds of the Senate being carryovers from previous elections) had a unenviable record of bitter partisan wrangling, passed little legislation, had seemingly unending fights over confirming Presidential appointments and budgets, and even voted to shut itself down for three weeks.

As a result, a November, 2013 Gallup poll found that Americans' approval of the way Congress handles its job was 9%, the lowest in Gallup's 39-year history of asking the question. The previous low was 10%, in 2012.

Americans are not in synch with their legislators' beliefs either. The best evidence we have (admittedly on a state legislative level but conducted across the nation) is a study published in the Atlantic Monthly, *What Politicians Believe About Their Constituents: Asymmetric Misperceptions and Prospects for Constituency Control*, (http://www.theatlantic.com/politics/archive/2013/03/are-americans-as-conservative-as-their-elected-officials-think/273669/) by political science graduate students David Broockman of Berkeley, and Christopher Skovron of the University of Michigan. .

The study showed that the opinions of nearly 2,000 state legislative candidates, when compared to actual district-level opinion based on other objective surveys routinely overestimated the ideological polarization of their constituents. "There is a striking conservative bias in politicians' perceptions, particularly among conservatives: conservative politicians systematically believe their constituents are more conservative than they actually are by more than 20 percentage points on average, and liberal politicians also typically overestimate their constituents' conservatism by several percentage points."

How Congress Drifted Out Of Touch With Its Constituents

So how did Congress get so out of touch with American public opinion?

> ► One reason is that the political views of the people who live in a district are less important for policy makers and policymaking than the power of organized political groups in a district. Republican organizational successes at the state level over the last

few decades have paid off in electing Republican state legislators. They have advanced a conservative agenda and put themselves into a position to gerrymander both state and U.S. House districts so Republicans get elected far in excess of their party strength, much as their "Dixiecrat" predecessors did for generations. Lopsided majorities of incumbents use their advantages to make electoral rules and districts that favor themselves and their allies.

▶ The power of groups with a strong conservative ideology like the Tea Party is thereby magnified and perpetuated even if only a minority of voters support their viewpoints. Since the districts are "safe" for the majority party, defeat in primary elections constitute the real threat for legislators. They court the highly-organized and ideological groups like the Tea Party. Candidates adopt a lot of their agenda using this strategy of agreement as a defensive tactic to fend off possible primary challenges from their right.

▶ Another reason is the conservative bias of past elections that took place under our staggered elections system. We only elect one third of the U.S. Senate at a time, leaving two thirds of the body to reflect the opinions of past elections and blunting any mandate that may have emerged at a given election.

▶ Also, constitutionally-mandated Senate districts mean effectively unequal Senate representation since all Senators run at large from the 50 states and the states are grossly unequal in population. For example, in 2012 a Senator from Wyoming represented a population of 576,412 while a Senator from California represented 38,041,430 people, giving Wyoming residents effectively 66 times more Senate representation than Californians.

▶ The most important reason for minority rule is the requirement of supermajorities to pass legislation or approve appointments. A supermajority requires support of a more than a majority of 50% plus one to pass legislation. This magnifies the power of majorities by giving them the power to effectively hold the body hostage by opposing something.

For example, if it takes two thirds to ratify a treaty, a minority of one third plus one will kill it. Under current U.S. Senate rules, a three-fifths (60%) majority is required to end a filibuster. The recent so-called "nuclear option" ended this practice for voting on Presidential appointments but not for legislation. To put this in perspective, though, in 2005, then-Senate Majority Leader Bill Frist called this idea "the constitutional option" when he came close to invoking it on behalf of the judicial nominees of President George W. Bush.

►   In most private bodies such as corporate boards and in most democratic parliamentary systems, supermajorities do not exist. Nor is it a U.S. constitutional requirement except in special cases, to override a presidential veto or ratify a treaty.

Political scientists Norman Ornstein and Thomas Mann in their book, *It's Even Worse Than It Looks: How the American Constitutional System Collided with the New Politics of Extremism*, (Basic Books, 2012), argued that congressional gridlock is mostly the fault of the right wing of the Republican Party who use supermajorities to engage in "policy hostage-taking" to extend their political war against the president.

They also say that mainstream media and media fact-checkers add to the problem by indulging in "false equivalency"—pretending both parties are equally to blame.

"Sadly, divided party government, which we have because of the Republican House, in a time of extreme partisan polarization, is a formula for inaction and absolutist opposition politics, not for problem solving," according to Mann.

Making Congress More Efficient

So what do we do about this?

They say women talk too much. If you have worked in Congress you know that the filibuster was invented by men.

—Clare Boothe Luce

Frankly, there is little that will establish majority rule in Congress without major constitutional change since separation of powers and staggered elections are built into the Constitution by design to effectively stymie majority rule. It works.

Still, short of major constitutional surgery, we can make a few changes that will improve things enough to get us out of gridlock and back to the "normal" Congressional dysfunction and bipartisanship that has plastered over Congressional divisions throughout most U.S. history.

- ► The main thing we can do is extend the "nuclear option" in the Senate by ending supermajorities except as required by the constitution. All it would take, Frist said when Republicans controlled the Senate, was for the presiding officer of the Senate (always a member of the majority party) to rule in favor of changing the rules to confirm on simple majority. If a simple majority voted to uphold that change, it would take effect. So doing would allow a simple majority to carry the day and disempower minorities of less than 50% until the next election.

- ► Another helpful rule change in the Senate would be to limit the time allotted to a filibuster to 72 hours. Enacting such a limitation would still provide sufficient time for a minority to plead its case but limit their ability to hold the rest of the body hostage. It might also increase the relevance of the debate.

- ► There is little that needs to be done in the House of Representatives because the constitution already makes it subject to frequent and complete elections and there are far fewer rules empowering minorities. Any major changes in the House would need to come from outside, e.g., outlawing of gerrymandering and reforming the campaign finance system.

- ► Along the same lines, enactment of public financing of Congressional campaigns and/or limiting the amount of money a special interest group can spend to influence elections would serve to limit the power of special interests to dominate elections, thereby magnifying the power of the majority of voters in elections for both houses of Congress.

Beyond these very modest reforms, to transform Congress into a democratic legislature that is held responsive to public opinion through periodic general elections and equal representation of each citizen would require sweeping constitutional change. The advisability and feasibility of this will be examined in a forthcoming chapter.

Chapter Fifteen

Reforming the Executive Branch

The executive branch of the United States has emerged as a massively powerful institution in the separation of powers system of the United States government. In a very real sense, it is the principal persona of the U.S. political system both domestically and internationally. The lynchpin of the branch is the elected President who, potentially, has almost unbridled power as head of state and commander-in-chief of the armed forces. Constitutionally, the chief executive is also charged with implementing and enforcing the laws written by Congress and has extensive patronage powers. A new President also has, in principle, the power to appoint more than 6,700 new federal positions (the people who work for the executive branch). In practice, the President and his transition and "insider" staff name about 1,200, including cabinet members, ambassadors, and U.S. Attorneys. Most appointments require Senate confirmation. (www.govspot.com/know/appointments). These positions are listed in the "Plum Book" (*United States Government Policy and Supporting Positions*), a Congressional publication which outlines appointive federal positions and is updated after each presidential election

During his or her tenure in office, the President also has the power to replace appointed officials who leave (subject to Congressional ratification) and, critically, nominate federal judges who serve for life unless removed for cause, which occurs rarely. This power encompasses judges for the United States District Courts, the United States Courts of Appeals, and the United States Supreme Court.

The Vice President is also part of the executive branch, ready to assume the Presidency should the need arise. Historically, vice presidents have had little power, although there have been significant exceptions including the last two VP's, Richard Cheney and Joseph Biden.

The Cabinet and the agencies behind cabinet members and the entire spectrum of independent federal agencies are also a big part of the executive branch. They are responsible for the day-to-day enforcement and administration of federal laws and ride herd over a diverse array of missions and constituencies in foreign and domestic policy.

A major component of the executive branch is the Executive Office of the President (EOP). It is a large bureaucracy which encompasses the immediate staff of the President and layers of support staff reporting to the White House. It is headed by the White House Chief of Staff and currently has about 1,800 official staffers but its real size and budget are shrouded in mystery because many people are detailed to it from other executive agencies. Staff estimates range from 2,000 to 6,000 employees with an annual budget between $300 million and $750 million.

Created in 1939 by Franklin D. Roosevelt to assist with administering a rapidly growing government in the wake of the New Deal, the EOP's mission is to advise the president. It has grown commensurately with the size of the U.S. government and its burgeoning responsibilities. Former EOP insider and historian Theodore Sorensen was quoted in the *Washington Post* as saying some presidents use the EOP "as a farm league, some use it as a source of experts and implementers, and some use it as Elba."

The Paradox of Presidential Power

Presidential power and the scope of the office has grown substantially over the span of U.S. history, but the power and scope of this highly-visible branch of the U.S. government is not without limits even in the era of the so-called imperial presidency. The paradox of the 21st century executive branch is that the presidency and the organization which surrounds it has both too much power in many areas to comfortably fit into a democratic form of government and too little power to govern effectively in a dangerous and complex world.

The overpowering side of the paradox is well known. The executive branch can do much by fiat without consulting the other branches of government or the American people because of its control of the vast bureaucracy and military. By a stroke of the pen or a voice over a secure telephone, the President can commit armed forces and issue sweeping executive orders to modify laws and regulations. The executive office also has an enormous ability to control the public agenda. Via press conferences, TV addresses and the "bully pulpit," this branch can and often does seize the agenda of public discourse by provoking a foreign or domestic policy crisis, proposing a major policy direction, or creating diversions to mask potentially controversial or embarrassing issues.

Albeit, the media counterbalances these massive powers to some degree by the intense scrutiny of the branch and has the potential to expose abuse. In practice, though, the ability of the media to exercise this counterbalance is limited because of government secrecy and the ability of the EOP to insulate inside decision-making from real-time media probing.

The limiting side of the paradox of presidential power is that the executive branch can be hamstrung by the other branches and the constitution.

One little-discussed limitation on presidential power is the issue of presidential transition. Since the office is so complex and requires not only having a team in place but the ability to understand the often obtuse and secret issues, to know who can be trusted and to learn how to make and promote policy, it usually takes a new administration a year or more to transition into the job of making effective public policy.

A glance at history shows that a majority of the huge blunders made by presidential administrations take place early in the first term when those in charge either overestimate their powers or underestimate the barriers to policy development and implementation.

The Congressional powers of investigating, budgeting, and legislating also have a limiting effect upon what the executive regimes are able to accomplish over the course of a term of office. Further limiting factors can be declining presidential popularity as reflected in public opinion polling. Presidents in their first term want to get reelected, and "lame duck" presidents in their second term want to leave a good historical legacy, advance their ideologies, and protect their party.

Another limitation on the executive branch is the sheer enormity of the long and expensive electoral road to the White House. Candidates must raise huge sums of money and literally campaign for years. During this gladiatorial-like process, they run the obstacle course of bruising primaries and contend with highly ideological electorates that do not reflect the electorate in general elections. Candidates are forced to take polarizing positions to win primaries. However, the positions they take to influence the electorate in the primary make them vulnerable to charges of extremism when they face the broader and more ideologically diverse November electorate.

In our political system, money is power. And that means a few can have a lot more power than the rest. That's bad news for everyone else–and for our democracy itself.

—Al Franken (U.S. Senator)

A corollary to this combative electoral experience is the effect the contemporary primary election system has on presidential popularity. Since a candidate must appeal to the party faithful who vote in primaries to secure votes at the nominating convention, he or she tends to be driven to the ideological center of the primary voters, i.e.., away from the moderate center. The new President comes into office with ideologically-driven pockets of supporters.

The realities of governing, however, tend to pull presidents toward compromise and the center. This dialectic leads to disappointment and withdrawal of active support from the very constituencies that got him/ her nominated. As the President loses support from key constituencies, he or she begins to appear weaker and more vulnerable, thereby limiting his or her power even more.

On the constitutional side, a serious limitation on executive branch power is the confirmation powers of the U.S. Senate. First, the unwritten but powerful practice of Senatorial Courtesy gives the senior Senator of the President's party in the relevant state or states covered by the appointment an important say in who is nominated and confirmed to a federal position. If the president bucks a powerful Senator, he or she runs the risk of losing key confirmation votes in the Senate. The 2014 Supreme Court decision that severely limited the power of the President to make recess appointments when Congress is not in session further exacerbates this limitation. Additionally, the persistently strong partisanship of the current era leads opponents of the President to block nominations based on party opposition rather than nominee qualifications.

Second, even with the requirement for a simple majority now in place to ratify nominations, mustering a majority of the Senate behind controversial or direction-changing presidential nominations can be difficult. In this era of aggressive partisanship, this has become a major stumbling block for Presidents who wish to put their own people in office and shape the federal judiciary and bureaucracy to their policy goals.

94

Another colossal limitation on presidential power is the 22nd amendment which limits a President to two four year terms. This mandate creates a massive focus on the next and only election for a new administration. This political myopia distracts attention from, and blurs the will to pursue controversial policies in order to secure good presidential polling numbers. Worse yet, once a reelected President becomes a lame duck, his or her power begins to ebb almost immediately. The executive is the only elected office subject to federal term limits. Not so parenthetically, term limitations are profoundly antithetical to a working democracy because they rob the electorate of the formidable restraining threat of defeat at the next election once a president becomes a lame duck after his re-election.

Proximate reforms

Frankly, most of what should be done to reform the executive branch, resolve the paradoxes of the institution, and make it more democratic requires major constitutional reform and will be covered in a later chapter.

Barring any major constitutional surgery, however, there are still a few things that can be done which will improve the democratic nature and efficiency of the office.

First on the agenda is reformation of how the President gets elected. Instead of working through political parties weakened and ideologically skewed by primary elections, the valuable role of political parties as aggregators and articulators of public opinion could be heightened by creating a single national presidential primary run by the national party rather than the state parties. This national electorate would marginalize ideological extremes because party factions across the entire nation would weigh in, canceling extremes found in narrow regions only. The legislation creating this primary should mandate that the top two or three vote-getters would automatically be nominated as candidates at their national party conventions.

Abolition of individual state primaries and the creation of a few regional primaries would accomplish the same thing, albeit less efficiently.

Taking away the power of states to run federal elections in their jurisdictions might require a constitutional amendment or at least be embodied in Congressional legislation and ratified by the court system. But however it is accomplished, it is a reform that is long overdue.

If we federalize federal elections and couple that with public financing of campaigns to limit the role of special interest money and wealthy minorities, it would make it easier and less expensive to run for President. It would also make it more likely that candidates who can appeal to the general electorate would emerge from the party conventions. The first step toward such an outcome would be to overturn the Citizens United vs. F.E.C. court decision which allows unlimited special interest spending. That in itself would likely encourage more people (particularly those without enormous wealth) to run. Additionally, it would take the onus off raising money and the placation of special interests that go along with that, and create more focus on the issues that are important to the electorate.

The problems of presidential transition probably cannot be avoided altogether because of the incredibly steep learning curve for this powerful office. The problem can be mitigated by increasing the ability of administrations to appoint people without waiting (often for years) for the Senate to ratify key people to serve in the administration. Long-time aides and staff could be more quickly brought on board, eliminating or at least dramatically shortening the time to learn who can be relied upon and who cannot.

This reform would also serve to make the Executive Office of the Presidency and the larger bureaucracy below it more responsive to administrations and ultimately to the electorate. This would obviate to a degree the ability of bureaucrats and interest groups to wait out the policies of a president they do not like because they would have to deal with presidential power applied more swiftly and surely.

The best weapon of a dictatorship is secrecy, but the best weapon of a democracy should be the weapon of openness.

—Niels Bohr

Another badly needed reform in the post-911 era is to limit spying, intelligence, and suspension of constitutionally-mandated civil liberties by an executive bureaucracy using the rationale of national security. Admittedly, there are real security issues to be addressed. The government's defense capability should not be hamstrung by the needed new legislation and legal interpretations that would balance the need for security and civil liberties more even-handedly.

On the other side of the ledger, widespread policy making through executive orders is not too worrisome to this analyst because the orders expire with the president and do not become enshrined in the permanent constitutional framework of the political system. In many cases, Presidents resort to this power because they have been frustrated by a legislative branch that has not passed a significant portion of the legislation that President has asked Congress to pass.

Creating a political environment that leads to more direct interaction between the President and Congress is also a good idea because it might lead to more cooperation. Extending the constitutional mandate for an annual State of The Nation address to Congress, Presidents should be required by newly-enacted legislation to make at least monthly in-person reports to joint sessions of Congress, following the example of parliamentary systems. Hopefully, this would be an interactive exchange creating a "question period" style of governing. This would increase the familiarity of both branches, if not more cooperation.

Another idea is to give the President the ability to fast-track legislation by requiring that it be voted upon by Congress within a year of proposal by the White House. This would require more efficient movement of legislation by Congress. Similarly, Congressional leaders should be made part of the deliberations of the Executive Office as policy is being made and not after the fact. Such involvement would give Congressional leaders more of a stake in getting legislation passed.

While these proximate reforms will do little to change the fundamental nature of the executive branch, they are a step in the direction of moderating some of the current problems. These basic reforms would alleviate the issue of an American executive with too much and too little power simultaneously and would ultimately lead to a less confrontational and better-organized national government.

Chapter Sixteen

The Federal Judicial System and Democracy

As we turn to the judicial leg of the three-legged separation of powers system of the U.S., a quick and general overview of the branch is in order since most Americans have little direct knowledge or interaction with the federal courts, and the news media usually limit themselves to analytical coverage on controversial Supreme Court decisions or confirmation hearings only and largely ignore lower court decision reporting, and provide little in the way of in-depth analysis of them.

The federal judicial branch has three principal levels and these include 94 district courts. Many district courts have more than one federal judge and sit at multiple locations. These courts are augmented by specialized courts dealing with bankruptcy, tax matters, claims against the federal government, intelligence, trade, and similar matters. Together, they constitute the basic civil and criminal trial court system.

Superseding the first judicial branch level are the 13 circuit courts. These courts are the first level of appeal from the district courts. Finally, The U.S. Supreme Court reigns over the whole system as the final referee in any legal dispute.

In addition, there are many federal officials with quasi-judicial authority created by statute. These include approximately 550 federal magistrates appointed to assist district court judges. They perform administrative duties by overseeing first appearances of criminal defendants, setting bail and the like. Unlike federal district judges, they serve eight-year terms for full-time positions, and four-year terms for part-timers, and may be reappointed. There are also many administrative and bankruptcy referees with quasi-judicial powers and duties scattered throughout the regulatory apparatus of the federal government.

Generally, federal courts, unlike state courts, are not courts of original jurisdiction, although there are exceptions. They have limited jurisdiction, hearing only cases authorized by the constitution, federal law, or treaties (the original jurisdiction powers). Cases involving state law fall under the federal court "diversity jurisdiction" doctrine. This doctrine allows civil plaintiffs from one state to file a federal lawsuit against a defendant from another state. The federal courts are used by the government to prosecute those charged with federal crimes.

In addition to the usual functions and jurisdictions mentioned above, there are many more nuances of jurisdiction and conflicts between state and federal courts that are too complex to enumerate in this context.

Turning to an analysis of the performance of the U.S. federal court system in our quasi-democratic system, an important and enduring principle of mainstream democratic political thought is that democratic governments need an independent judiciary to protect rights, settle disputes, and offer an alternative to the violent settlement of conflicts. An impartial, apolitical group of trusted "umpires" with established authority has been a bulwark of every successful democratic political system in history

The writers of the U.S. constitution tried to insure the independence of the federal judicial system by requiring Senate confirmation of candidates after they are nominated by the President, and by bestowing lifetime tenure to federal judges. The latter insulates them from the electoral process. In contrast, Political Scientist Larry Sabato writes in a 2010 Britannica blog, that state judges exist in an environment of "tawdry contests in states that put their supreme courts and various judicial posts on the ballot." How independent can judges be if they, as candidates, raise money from the very interests they are likely to judge?

In general, we need a strong and independent court system. As sensible as the general organization of the federal judicial branch seems, it is not perfect.

The two major troublesome issues of the federal judiciary that I believe should be addressed which will limit the undemocratic powers of the federal judiciary while still maintaining its independence are lifetime terms and the power of judicial review.

Presidents come and go, but the Supreme Court goes on forever.

—William Howard Taft (U.S. President)

The Lifetime Term Issue

Judges appointed by a president and confirmed by a Senate majority from a different era can serve for decades. The lifetime appointment of federal judges is mitigated somewhat by the fact that they can be removed from office if impeached and convicted by the Congress for alleged wrongdoings. Since this has only happened 14 times in the entire span of U.S. history, it is a deterrent with few teeth.

The high likelihood of a lifetime tenure raises the issue that some long-serving judges may fail to keep up with social and technical change as a matter of choice because they have no incentive to do otherwise. Also, as they age, long-serving judges can suffer the mental infirmities that eventually plague most people.

Since electing judges is not a good idea because judges hold the unique and necessary position of impartial umpire, we should turn to other means to limit lifetime appointments to avoid some of the disadvantages.

While I am strongly opposed to term limits for elected offices (my case will be made in a later chapter on elections), limits do make some sense for a non-elected office. Such limits have worked well for federal magistrates who are selected by district judges and who serve a specified term. This practice could work equally well for federal judges at all levels.

I am suggesting a constitutional change which would give federal judges terms of at least eight and perhaps twelve years. Such term limits would span a minimum of two full presidential terms and several senatorial election cycles, thereby making it difficult for a President to pack the court to his or her advantage. This would mitigate some of the problems of lifetime terms while still maintaining judicial independence. Sitting judges would have terms that carry over into the term(s) of the President following the one that appointed them, thereby insuring some independence. However, if a sitting judge is deemed valuable by a future president and Senatorial majority, he or she could be reappointed for another term.

Another way to ensure judicial independence is to take the common law doctrine of giving federal judges total immunity from personal liability for their judicial acts and enact it into law. Judges could still be removed by impeachment and conviction for wrongdoing.

I agree with Sabato, who pointed out in his essay that, "Absent a term limit, which would be my preference, the nation might want to consider a generous mandatory retirement age." This requirement might induce more judges to retire instead of dying in office.

The Power of Judicial Review

While we need federal judges to be neutral and fair umpires, we do not need them to act as an unelected legislature. Yet, that is precisely what they do when they exercise the power of judicial review, i.e., the power of judges to overturn and invalidate an act of Congress, the executive branch, or of state and local government. This most controversial power of federal courts is not included in the written portion of the U.S. Constitution. Only 11 of the 55 delegates to the Constitutional Convention were in favor of it, according to the notes of James Madison. It was seized by the U.S. Supreme Court in 1803 in Marbury vs. Madison, and this power to legislate has been enshrined into U.S. constitutional tradition ever since. It is time to un-enshrine it.

Extending far beyond the power to decide cases, this power has been yielded to frustrate majorities at critical junctures of American history, such as in the issues of slavery, the regulation of interstate commerce, and the "New Deal" legislation adopted in the wake of the Great Depression. In practical terms, the people, acting through their elected legislature, were thusly denied their right to make public policy.

If we truly want a democratic political system, we need to severely restrict if not abolish the power of non-elected officials to overturn the laws that those elected to govern have enacted. If the American people wish to revise their stance on future controversial issues as they have done on such issues as gay rights, racial segregation, and the consumption of liquor, they will have the power do so.

Judges should determine whether statutes apply to a given case but not whether the statutes themselves are constitutional. By definition in a democratic system, those who are constitutionally elected should have the final authority because they represent the people's will in a fair electoral system. Further, they can be removed from office if they make policies or act in ways that the people oppose.

Beyond these two major reforms, there are a few other things that are likely to improve the functioning of the federal court system.

One obvious reform is to appoint more judges and magistrates so that the backlog of cases that frequently exists in the courts' docket can be whittled down to size. The right to a speedy trail is enshrined in criminal law and it should also extend to civil law so cases do not drag on for long periods. Along these lines, the refusal of the Senate to confirm federal judicial candidates for partisan political reasons should be stopped by mandating an up or down vote within a year or less, preferably less. This practice, however, is a fault of the Senate, not the judicial system and needs to be addressed by Congressional reforms.

Also, the powers of special courts such as the Foreign Intelligence Surveillance Court should be enhanced and made more equitable by including into the process the testimony of advocates for civil liberties.

Given the huge burden of cases and issues faced by the U.S. Supreme Court, it makes sense to expand the court to more than nine judges. With additional judges more issues can be covered. The court would be able to work on more issues simultaneously through a division of labor. Increasing the number of sitting judges would not require a constitutional amendment since the U.S. Constitution does not specify how many judges should sit on the Supreme Court. Article 3, Section 1, specifies that there will be a Supreme Court. Article 1, Section 3, mentions the Chief Justice, and Article 2, Section 2, mentions the "Judges of the Supreme Court." Aside from these constitutional references there is neither a mandate on number of judges specified nor a limit to the size of the Supreme Court.

Bringing more public scrutiny to the judicial process also is a reform that makes sense for the federal courts, especially the appellate courts. In a survey conducted in 2010 by Fairleigh Dickinson University, it was found that the public's view on a more open court is evolving. Survey respondents, by a margin of 61% to 26%, said that "televising Supreme Court hearings would be good for democracy, rather than undermining the [Court's] dignity or authority." Democrats, Republicans, and Independents all were in the majority on this question.

Again turning to Sabato on the subject of federal court reform, he wrote in the essay cited above, "Inevitably, these reforms will have political consequences, although they are not immediately predictable. So what? The political nature of the Court has been on display at the confirmation hearings of every recent appointee, and even at the 2010 State of the Union address....the Court is naturally political—and it does not reside on Mount Olympus."

Decisions such as the 5-4 majorities in Bush vs. Gore in 2000, and The Citizens United vs. The Federal Elections Commission in 2008, certainly affirm Sabato's views. Despite judicial independence and lifetime appointments, the adage (first promulgated by journalist Finley Peter Dunne in 1901) which states that the Supreme Court follows electoral returns has a ring of truth to it. So the opinion that reforms to make the court more open would make the court more political are moot. The court is and will remain a political instrument because of its pivotal role in the political system. It is time we treated it as such.

Chapter Seventeen

Democracy and Elections in the United States

Elections are crucial for any democratic political system. No democratic political system can exist without free and fair elections. The very existence of elections is so widely thought to offer legitimacy to a political system that many authoritarian, non-democratic nations hold sham or mock elections and thereby claim democratic legitimacy. Elections are offered as proof that these nations are responsive to their citizens. Responsible political analysts are not fooled by such pseudo-democratic shenanigans: the mere act of voting does not constitute a democracy.

Truly democratic elections must meet minimum criteria:

► They must be open to all, allowing any adult citizen to run for office and vote a secret ballot without fear of retaliation from those in power or those lurking behind the scenes.

► The campaign playing field must be level. Candidates and groups of candidates (political parties and interest groups) must be allowed to assemble. They must be able to say what they want to convince people to vote for them. The news media must be free and unfettered. If either certain utterances or subjects are not allowed or, if those who bring them up have a legitimate fear of retaliation from those in power, then the freedom of speech, assembly, and press associated with fair elections does not exist.

► Elections must be meaningful. Those who win get to take the reins of government for a set period. Those who are defeated must relinquish their power since the people have spoken. If referenda are involved, they should become law if passed.

► Ballots must be counted fairly and electoral fraud or voter suppression cannot be tolerated in any manner in a democratic election.

► Very importantly, genuine democratic elections must be general, i.e., they must allow for the entire policy-making apparatus of the government to be elected instead of keeping many in power because they are not on the ballot and not subject to popular control. The judiciary should be an exception to this because their role is to referee policy rather than to make it.

If Congress can move President's Day, Columbus Day and, alas, Martin Luther King's Birthday celebration for the convenience of shoppers, shouldn't they at least consider moving Election Day for the convenience of voters?

—Andrew Young

If these minimal criteria are met, citizens in a democracy have a tremendously effective mechanism to select their government. Simultaneously, a compelling incentive will be created for those elected to govern with public opinion in mind since they risk being voted out at the next election if they do not.

Democracy in U.S. Elections

Elections in the United States of America have many democratic elements but, unfortunately, elections fall short on several important levels. Let's examine each one and evaluate some reforms that would make our political system more democratic.

Parenthetically, so far in this book, I have advocated proximate, largely non-constitutional reforms. Elections are so critical to democracy that they mark a critical turning point toward more extensive reforms. Such reforms require fairly significant departures from U.S. constitutional practices. Moreover, some constitutional provisions to make U.S. elections more democratic also require a lot of "ordinary" legislation and policy-making to buttress national elections to meet these criteria in every state. A few examples follow:

▶ Open Access: The United States does an excellent job of allowing open access to elections in the 21st century. Certain jurisdictions historically have discriminating laws and policies designed to prevent certain racial and ethnic groups from voting or running for office. Most of these laws have been erased by federal law. Today, just about anybody of any racial or ethnic background or of any ideology can file to be a candidate for political office or to vote, although it still remains difficult in a few jurisdictions.

- ▶ Free Marketplace of ideas: The nation also does a commendable job of protecting a free press and fostering a lively environment of public policy debate. No major reforms are needed in this area, although Americans need to be constantly on guard to threats aimed at a free press and a free marketplace of ideas, especially those driven by and cloaked in the guise of national security.

- ▶ Level Playing Field: Far less satisfactory is the U.S. performance in creating a level playing field for candidates. Money controls the success of a candidate to broadcast h/his message. Special interests groups dominate elections by contributing the lion's share of this money. This practice has accelerated in the wake of the 2010 Citizens United v The Federal Elections Commission decision of the U.S. Supreme Court. The decision held that the first amendment prohibits the government from restricting independent political expenditures by corporations, associations or labor unions. This decision has exacerbated the role of money in politics and the recent trend for special interests not officially affiliated with candidates or parties to spend massive amounts to try to influence elections. According to opensecrets.com (Center for Responsive Politics), $6,285,557,223 was spent on the 2012 national elections. Of that amount, $2,621,415,792 was spent on the Presidential race. This compares to $3,643,942,915 spent in 2010 Congressional elections and $5,285,680,883 spent in the 2008 election with $2,799,728,146 going to the Presidential race. The totals in 2000 were just a little over three billion dollars.

Much of this money went to fund negative ads run against candidates and parties by so-called independent and/or social welfare groups who do not have to disclose their donors and, by law, cannot coordinate their campaigns with candidates. The same source reports that campaign contributions of $200 or more were given by only four-tenths of one percent of the population. Eight-tenths of a percent of the population contributed $2,500 or more. Clearly, the wealthy and their groups are dominating the political debate.

Do the math on the amount spent on Congressional elections. Unless a candidate for the U.S. legislative house has the ability to raise millions of dollars to counter this massive special interest spending, he or she has little chance of being elected to office.

National party committees give their strong support only to those who can raise a lot of money.

What can be done to level the playing field and allow more competitive races? One thing that would help is effectively repealing Citizens United v FEC by requiring special interest campaigns to make their donors public while simultaneously tightening the rules against the coordination of campaigns and independent expenditures. Too many "independent" political action committees and so-called social welfare groups are thinly and artificially separated from parties and candidates. The FEC needs to vigorously enforce existing laws against this practice and Congress needs to make the separation requirements far more stringent.

A reform that would go far toward leveling the playing field and limit the need for candidates to beg for campaign funds from special interests would be the enactment and funding significant public financing of all federal campaigns. Once candidates qualify to run, they should be given access to sum of public money sufficient to ensure that their message can be delivered to the electorate via the media.

As a condition of their license to hold a government-enforced monopoly to use a part of the scarce broadcast frequency spectrum to make money by selling commercial time for their programming, broadcast stations should be required to donate a reasonable and equal amount of on-air campaign time to all federal candidates, thereby extending the impact of public financing of campaigns.

Licensed broadcast media should provide candidates sufficient air time to reach the electorate via the repetition practiced in modern advertising. Newspapers and other print and Internet media who do not have access to such a monopoly should be given tax incentives for providing free space to all federal candidates.

To make this even more meaningful, campaign total spending limits should be enacted to limit the amount of money spent beyond the public financing funds that parties, campaigns and special interests are allowed to influence an election, whether the spending was coordinated or not. That would discourage "independent expenditures" and make U.S. federal elections more competitive.

▶ Meaningful Electoral Impact: The U.S. does quite well at ensuring that those who win federal elections actually serve in the office they have won. The glaring exception to this involves the existence of the Electoral College and its allocation of all votes in a state to a candidate who might have won only 50.1% of a large state. Several times in U.S. history, the candidate who received the majority of votes in a presidential election did not get to serve as President. John Q. Adams, Rutherford Hayes and William Harrison became the President this way. In the 2000 election, Al Gore got 542,816 more votes than George W. Bush, yet Bush was elevated to the Presidency by the U.S. Supreme Court.

▶ Even if the allegation that the Electoral College made sense in 1789 due to widespread voter illiteracy as stipulated, this is certainly not true in the 21st century. If we are serious about democracy, we need to abolish the Electoral College.

▶ We need to count the votes nationally for this national office and ensure that the candidate who gets the most votes gets the office. If nobody receives a majority, a runoff election can be held, as in most democracies. The argument that this would reduce the influence of smaller states is probably true but is not relevant. People vote, and lines drawn on a map are not citizens and should have no voting rights. A majority is a majority, no matter where in America people reside. Each vote should count and be counted equally, and that does not happen with the Electoral College in place.

▶ Fair counting of ballots: The United States has a spotty record on equally granting the right to vote and the accurate counting of ballots. Voting irregularities in cities and states have long been alleged and uncovered.

There is also a long history of voter suppression laws and tactics going back to the era of literacy tests, poll taxes, and other ways to discourage black people form voting in the South. Politicians who use gerrymandering to secure and perpetuate their stranglehold by discouraging minorities and other populations to vote who are inclined to support the opposing party are guilty of this practice although few admit it. These practices which have continued into the present have been promulgated by mostly, but certainly not exclusively, Republican legislatures and governors because they control so many states now.

Since elections are controlled by the states under the present constitution, we need at a minimum a new Federal Voting Rights Act that would outlaw gerrymandering in any electoral district and outlaw voter suppression laws and policies in all states. To give this law real teeth, a constitutional amendment that gives the federal government the right to run elections would be very helpful.

► General Elections: On this criterion, the U.S. political system fails woefully. This flaw is due to the separation of powers and the system of checks and balances built into the U.S. Constitution. This was designed by the writers of constitution who feared giving the people too much say in the new nation. Consequently, they designed an electoral system to prevent general elections. There has never been an election when the American people can vote to elect (or unelect) a government. Americans vote for the U.S. House of Representatives every two years. Two-thirds of the Senate are always holdovers from the previous election so the voters can never change the Congress in one election. We can vote for the President and Vice President every other election but because of term limits, we can re-elect the President only one time. This stricture leaves the president a lame duck after successful re-election, effectively removing the threat of voter disapproval for the remainder of the term.

To really transform our elections into true general elections, we would have to abolish the Presidential term limits (enacted after Franklin Roosevelt's tenure) in the 22nd amendment and change Congressional terms so we would vote for all members of Congress (both houses) at the same time as the President and Vice President.

Since there is nothing sacred about two year election cycles, we could easily change the election cycle to three or four years which would also have the beneficial effect of making it less costly for House of Representatives members who have to raise money for elections every two years, thereby creating a virtually permanent fund-raising task for them.

Chapter Eighteen

Improving U.S. Elections:
Increasing Participation, Lowering Costs
and Securing Results

As we have seen, fair and open elections that meet the criteria for democratic voting are a critical component of any functioning democracy. Whether the purpose of a given election is to transform a slate of candidates into governors for a given period, or to provide a policy mandate through referenda, democracies cannot work without a functioning and fair electoral system. As this analysis makes the turn toward some fundamental and sweeping recommendations about ways to improve the democratic performance of elections in the United States of America, we need to recognize that all elections function within a political system and cannot be separated from the cultural expectations and practices of their environment.

Rather than viewing any given election in isolation, sound political analysis requires an understanding of the entire election process. The real time activity of casting and counting ballots is not merely a single event that takes place on Election Day. Rather, it is the zenith of an ongoing process that can take as long as several years and evolves with culture and technology.

Running and Campaigning

The democratic electoral process begins with the decision to run for public office or to formulate a policy via a referendum. A candidate for a given public office kicks off the process by throwing his or her proverbial hat into the ring, usually after testing the waters and lining up potential support. In the case of an affiliated slate, a candidate must become part of a political party and let potential voters know that he or she desires their support—and contributions through party channels and through individual campaign channels. In the contemporary era, the latter is usually dominant.

Referenda to create public policies begin along a similar path by starting with a person or a group that decides that it wants people to vote for a policy proposition. Referenda, particularly those that challenge social norms over such issues as gay marriage or marijuana legalization, can become very controversial and draw massive and expensive campaigns funded by organized groups.

Even though polling data over time show that Americans do not hold a high opinion of politics and politicians (those who make up a major part of what is called political culture), we do not have a serious shortage of candidates desiring to run for office or those who want to see a referendum on the ballot. Consequently, little needs to be done to encourage more candidates to come forward in competitive districts although the qualifications of those candidates are sometimes marginal. The only exception is that there is a shortage of serious candidates in very non-competitive districts and some state and local candidates run unopposed and are elected by default.

If we make running for, and serving in, public office more desirable, it is likely that we would attract more qualified people to enter politics. If we can attract more and better candidates in all districts by finding ways to make more districts more competitive and limiting the exorbitant costs of campaigning, we will be on the road to improving the public's perception of politics and government while improving the way our political system operates.

Under the present system, those who do decide to run for office have a long and difficult path to mount a credible campaign and have a fighting chance of getting elected. Once their hat is thrown in the ring, candidates immediately face the often-significant hurdles of securing a place on the ballot before they can actually stand for election. Signatures of registered voters on a petition must be gathered and/or a sometimes-steep filing fee must be raised and given to the electoral authorities. Candidate qualification requirements are often very exacting and must be strictly followed to qualify. Even the most minor deviation can result in a candidate being disqualified.

With the exception of non-partisan local and state elections, candidates have to make almost immediate decisions about what party affiliation they declare. Even in many non-partisan elections, the de facto support of local party machines is thrown behind those who have been members and supporters of the party machine.

Candidates also need to decide what they stand for and what platform items they will emphasize as they run for office. The only exception to this is in very small towns where the people personally know those who want to run and what they stand for as candidates.

From the moment they decide to run for office, candidates face the need to organize and fund a long and often very expensive campaign if they want to be serious competitors. Every detail must be on the agenda including but not limited to planning how to recruit volunteers, how and when to contact voters, and how to develop strategy and collect resources to implement an effective "get-out-the-vote" campaign.

As part of the campaign strategy, candidates also need to consider, among other things, how they approach on the issues of the day in a given election, and the best methods of delivering the campaign message. They also need to consider the best ways to determine and track public opinion (polling) and of identifying and recruiting capable people in the areas of campaign strategy, organization, media relations, advertising, and voter turnout (commonly referred to as "the ground game").

For these and a myriad of other matters, professional help is commonly sought for all but purely local races in advance of officially announcing one's candidacy for public office. All of this takes money—usually a lot of money.

If the candidate is fortunate, no candidate from the same party will run for the same position nor will the candidate have to contend with more candidates than there are positions in a non-partisan race and, therefore, he or she can avoid a primary. Frequently though, there are other candidates running and one election becomes two and the cost and complexity of a campaign is thereby greatly increased.

Unfortunately, primary elections not only dramatically increase the cost of running for office by forcing candidates to run two elections with two different electorates and very different strategies for victory, but they often divide parties by casting one group of a party or viewpoint against another with similar political affiliations.

Candidates are making lasting impressions on voters, not just primary voters, in how they campaign.

—Jeb Bush

Improving Elections by Limiting Primaries

A far better solution for screening an oversupply of candidates would be the abolition of primaries by instituting a simple majority requirement for election. If no candidate gets a majority of the vote, a runoff between the top two vote-getters should be held. Instead of all elections having two parts, only the few involving runoffs would be doubled under such a system.

Campaigning for the office of President of the U.S., in particular, is both frightfully expensive and begins years before an actual election. State after state holds caucuses, primary elections, party nominating conventions, and so forth, thereby forcing candidates to raise huge sums of money and run for years at a time. As I suggested earlier, it would be more sensible to limit this electoral process by holding a single national Presidential primary, or just a few regional primaries to pick the candidates.

An even better solution would be to abolish Presidential primaries and let the parties nominate their candidates at national conventions, and allow all so nominated to run in a national election. The use of the run-off system will lead to selecting a candidate who can muster a national majority of votes. Parties who want to field candidates who have a chance to win will be led to consider the desires of the national electorate instead of catering to the agendum of a highly partisan primary electorate. In this way, parties will tend to nominate candidates who favor positions held by the majority of the electorate instead of yielding to the ideologically pure positions that can influence a primary electorate and attract special interest money. Congressional elections should follow a similar process.

Running and winning are only part of the democratic electoral cycle, of course. If a candidate is elected, the process continues with changing the guard, so to speak. Winners prepare for actually taking office. They must appoint subordinates, create plans to implement pledges made during the campaigns, etc. Those who did not win need to commit to the process despite their dismay at the result. Democracy requires that all support or at least accept the election results. Coups d'état or refusals to recognize fair election results are antithetical to democracy.

Improving Elections By Increasing Turnout

Turning to other ways to improve U.S. elections, an increase in voter turnout would make the system more responsive to public opinion.

Although voting rights have been secured for all citizens by the Voting Rights Act and other federal acts, voter turnout (the portion of the eligible electorate that actually votes) is still quite low in many jurisdictions. While Presidential elections usually have at least a small majority of potential voters casting ballots, that is not the case for many Congressional elections in non-Presidential election years and certainly not the case for many state and, especially, local elections.

While some of the low turnout can be attributed to the American political culture's deprecation of the legitimacy and worth of government and politics, one of the major causes for low voter turnout can be attributed to the fact that elections are inconvenient for voters. Controlled as they are by the 50 states, some of which give subjurisdictions like counties and cities the right to make their own electoral rules, elections traditionally are held on a Tuesday and run for about 12 hours. While absentee ballots and early voting (often at very inconvenient locations) are allowed in some jurisdictions, there is little uniformity involved. Moreover, some states require potential voters to register as much as 30 days in advance and to provide many forms of identification to register and to vote.

Again, as I have suggested, if elections were held at more convenient times and voting in general was more convenient as is the case in many democratic countries, turnout would increase. To accommodate those who work during the week, I recommend that the voting polls be open at least on the weekends as well as weekdays for a period encompassing a minimum of several days. To make voting less inconvenient, using the ability of computer systems to verify identity, as it is currently employed for the issuance of firearm permits or driver licenses, the day-of-voting registration should be universally implemented. The use of real time computers would further accommodate those who are motivated by the media and/or campaigns to participate, which often occurs during the last few days before an election as campaigns reach high levels of intensity.

Further, now that computer security has been perfected to the point that banks and financial institutions routinely use online transactions with high levels of safety and people can buy goods online with as much security as in-store buying, voting via the Internet should be allowed. Voters could then register their preferences from the comforts of their homes or offices. This would avoid having to make a special trip to the polls and the irksome need of standing in line at a voting place.

Improving Elections by Outlawing Gerrymandering and Lowering Election Costs

Another important way to increase voter turnout in U.S. elections is to increase their competitiveness. Many people do not vote because they feel that the results are predetermined and their vote will not affect the outcome. Incumbents have a huge advantage over challengers and are able to raise enormous sums of money from interest groups. High electoral costs make it tough for challengers to raise enough money for truly competitive campaigns. Reinforcing this edge is the common practice of majorities in state legislature to gerrymander districts by manipulating district boundaries to favor those who vote for incumbents and the majority party.

As mentioned earlier, to ameliorate these problems, campaign spending and contribution limits should be enacted, accompanied by the public financing of elections and/or public access to the airwaves and other media for candidates to get the campaign message to the voters. These changes would even the playing field and help to motivate potential voters to exercise their right to vote.

With these changes and the enhancement of a strictly-enforced federal law that makes gerrymandering a crime bolstered by the empowerment of the Federal Elections Commission to overrule state districts if district lines are deemed to be drawn to favor one party over another, American elections would be more competitive and voter turnout should be higher.

Another probable cause for low turnout can be attributed to election fatigue and campaign nastiness. Driven by long campaigns fueled by unlimited campaign expenditures from both parties and so-called independent groups, campaigns engage in advertising that not only talks about goals but attacks the opponents. Since freedom of speech is important to campaigns and a basic American right, it would be anti-democratic to prohibit any type of campaign. However, placing limits on the duration of campaigns and the dollars spent for them would likely limit negative ads and alleviate voter fatigue.

Ultimately, democracy is served when it is easier for ordinary citizens to run for public office, to have the ability to run a credible campaign or to raise issues for public discussion, and for the electorate to vote.

Improving Democratic Elections by Making Votes Count

One of the fundamental principles of democracy that has emerged out of centuries of democratic thought and practical experience is that each vote needs to count and be given equal weight. If the candidate, party, or group that wins the most votes is denied the elected office or is removed from office by other than constitutional means such as impeachment or felony conviction in the U.S., then democracy is denied.

Unfortunately, as we have seen, the Electoral College system of the U.S. has led to several Presidential candidates in our history being denied the office they won. The last time was only 14 years ago when the U.S. Supreme Court ruled that George W. Bush become the President despite the undisputed fact that Al Gore got more votes. If we Americans are serious about democracy, the Electoral College system must be abolished. The constitution should be amended to secure the right of the *national* winner of any national federal election to occupy the position in the elected office. This would be analogous to awarding the office to the candidate who gets the most votes in U.S. House or Senate election.

While this change might decrease the influence of some small states on Presidential elections, that is not a problem because it is fully consistent with democracy. Lines on a map are abstractions and should not have the power of citizens or have influence on democratic and human rights. The people alone should be the recipients of these rights.

Chapter Nineteen

Moving Towards the Tricentennial
Creating a 21st Century Democratic America
with a Democratic Reform Agenda

Up to this point, we have evaluated the democratic performance of the United States government and suggested some limited reforms that fall well short of major constitutional surgery. Practically speaking, given the overwhelming built-in resistance to change of our separation of powers system, what we have proposed so far may be all we can hope to accomplish. The silver lining is that if we enact enough incremental reforms, collectively they may constitute a significant mid-course correction in the direction of democracy, bringing us closer to that desirable goal even if we don't reach it.

The advantages of proceeding this way are clear: they are achievable within the framework of our current political system and consistent with the general American constitutional traditions and political culture that have emerged to date. The important and undeniable disadvantage, though, is that the U.S. political system would still remain only partially democratic—without general elections—and, therefore, severely limit the power of a majority of citizens to unite around a given idea or political approach and change the government. Still lacking in the political system of the United States would be a basic principle of democracy, the ability of citizens to "throw the bums out" in an election. Without that, there is no mechanism to force those in power to pay more than lip service to public opinion and needs.

A Desirable Solution: Modernizing the Constitution While Retaining Our National Values

A constitution is a special entity and should not be tinkered with lightly. Far more than simply a written document, it is the sum total of widely-held political traditions that bind people together into a nation. As such, it is an evolving compilation of the rules, mores, court decisions, deep-seated political beliefs, and behavioral norms that guide a nation. It is a set of rules by which all other rules must conform.

Nevertheless, if we are serious about democratic change we would need to cross the proverbial Rubicon of major constitutional change by significantly modifying the U.S. Constitution so as to make it more hospitable to democracy.

Changing the U.S. Constitution in a democratic direction would neither be an easy task, given the deeply-rooted support for our republican form of government and the popularly held American belief that we already are a democracy, nor would it be a risk-free path. A panoply of special interests would surely emerge and demand their changes be enacted in the new amendments once the Pandora's Box of constitutional change has been opened.

The looming specter of a constitutional convention with shrill and sharply opposing interests would emerge. The interest groups who demand changes on firearms, criminal sentences, taxation changes, drug regulation, abortion and states' rights provisions will most likely enter the debate and be represented at the convention directly or indirectly. The presence of these groups, along with a large contingent of balanced budgeters and anti-immigration nativists, just to name a few of the more obvious factions in U.S. politics, each demanding that *their* changes be incorporated in a revised constitution, is a frightening prospect. What might emerge could steer the U.S. political system in a far different direction than democracy. Therefore, great care would have to be taken to limit the agenda of any vehicle for democratic change such as a constitutional convention or other mechanisms such as Congressional enactment or court interpretations to the democratic subject at hand, lest things get out of control and even lead to the sort of armed insurrection that Thomas Jefferson discussed in a Nov. 13, 1787, letter to William Stephens Smith. Writing about Shay's Rebellion in Massachusetts, Jefferson said, "…And what country can preserve its liberties if their rulers are not warned from time to time that their people preserve the spirit of resistance?…The tree of liberty must be refreshed from time to time with the blood of patriots and tyrants."

While scholars debate whether the Jefferson words were meant literally or metaphorically, it is clear that he felt that the constitutional order should and must be challenged. Each generation has the right to change the rules to suit its needs. Clearly, while I am sympathetic to this approach to change, somehow we must find a way to make limited changes by forging amendments that move the system closer to the ideal of democracy, the norm that underlies this book.

A More Democratic Constitution Envisioned

Thus, in the Jeffersonian spirit and chastened by a bit of fear toward unbridled change, it is a worthy exercise to consider what a more democratic U.S. political system might look like if far-reaching democratic changes in the constitutional framework were enacted.

Placing this in context, the U.S. Constitution has changed dramatically since its ratification in 1789 and the changes continue. Since 1789, there have been 27 written amendments and thousands of court decisions and collective national experiences and perceptions that have changed this steadily evolving set of principles. Some of this change has already been in a democratic direction. We have enfranchised women, abolished race and property qualifications for voting, enacted the direct election of the U.S. Senate (albeit with staggered terms), and moved appointment of members of the Electoral College from the state legislatures to the popular vote, albeit with a winner-take-all approach and no guarantees.

Despite these democratic changes, the original founders' model of a republic (a non-monarchy) has not been changed. While the current U.S. Constitution certainly has democratic elements such as the election of the entire House of Representatives every two years, and has mandated universal enfranchisement of citizens, full democracy remains elusive. By definition, the U.S. political system is not a true representative democracy because of the critical absence of general elections. At no time in the electoral cycle does a national election occur. Americans have never seen a ballot that allows them to vote on every national public official in their jurisdiction and thereby collectively vote a government slate of candidates in or out of office. Instead, separation of powers and staggered elections reigns and insulates two thirds of the powerful U.S. Senate and the President every other election from public opinion and voting behavior.

So what would a more democratic constitution look like?

In broad strokes, the changes needed are to abolish, or to fundamentally modify the components of the separation of powers that frustrate democratic elections. The founders put these provisions into the original document because they did not trust human nature. They believed that only elite power could check elite power since the citizens did not have the wisdom, training, or temperament to check government power. This stricture is even more anti-democratic when it is placed into the context

121

of the enfranchised electorate of the day that was restricted to white, male property owners.

A strong case for changing this entire governing approach can be made. Regardless of any justification of the founders' views about the 18th century electorate, it is demonstrable that the 21st century electorate is larger, far more representative of the population, better educated, has access to more information and, therefore, are at least as qualified as elites to check power. A democratic people should have that opportunity.

Here is my proposal for a hybrid constitutional system that would create general elections while preserving essential elements of the U.S. Constitution:

- ▶ **Free Speech needs to be free.** First, the basic rights of speech and press assembly, already in the constitution, must be reiterated and extended so elections are freer. Without the access to the free market of ideas that these basic political freedoms create, minorities cannot possibly hope to become majorities. So America needs a constitutional amendment that would unequivocally repeal Citizens United and any similar court decisions or legislation that equate paid speech with free speech which allow unlimited constitutional spending.

- ▶ **We need to diminish the effect of money in politics.** By replacing our present campaign finance system with an effective public financing of campaigns and limiting the amount of money any campaign or special interest can spend to influence any election to an amount just sufficient to get the message out to those who choose to listen, we could level the campaign playing field and reduce the impact of special interests on electoral outcomes, whether for a candidate or an issue. This may sound counterintuitive but it is not. By placing these restrictions on campaign financing and special interest spending, we would be creating more political freedom to campaign effectively irrespective of wealth, rather than less freedom.

- ▶ **We need an independent judiciary who represents the present generation.** We need to continue to maintain an independent federal judiciary without making it an unelected legislature with life tenure. The removal of judicial power to repeal acts of other branches and a term limit of 12 years for judges, as previously discussed, would go a long way toward redirecting the judiciary to a sensible role of acting as final referees in criminal and civil issues. Federal judges would become genuine constitutional interpreters instead of constitutional policy makers and holdovers from previous governments. Alternatively, we could limit the sweep of judicial review power of courts by allowing Congressional overrides on constitutional decisions by a simple majority.

▶ **We must abolish minority vetoes.** Extraordinary majorities, e.g., more than 50% of a body plus one, exaggerate the power of minorities. This gives minorities veto power over majorities. This practice is by its very nature profoundly undemocratic. All extraordinary majority requirements should be abolished for Congressional voting. A simple majority should be used to pass legislation, ratify treaties, confirm appointments, and cut off debate. To fail to uphold the majority vote is to provide the minority with more power than the majority. This practice, by definition, is not democratic.

▶ **We need to create general elections for Congress.** It is critical for democracy that we elect the entire Congress in a general election every four years. We can accomplish this by extending the terms of members of the House of Representatives to four years, cutting Senate terms back to four years and abolishing staggered Senate elections.

For House members, this would alleviate the constant focus on re-election and fundraising. While four-year terms would force Senators to campaign more frequently, the special powers of treaty ratification, confirmation (or rejection) of Presidential appointees which must take place within a maximum of 60 days, and similar powers would be preserved.

▶ **We should make the Senate more democratic.** The Senate should be enlarged and reapportioned to make it a more representative body. If we double the Senate size to 200 and elect all Senators nationally, we would remove representation by arbitrary territorial delineations and firmly establish equal representation of American people everywhere rather than representation by the dictates of state lines which are more accidents of history than cohesive groupings of population.

If the strict anti-gerrymandering law advocated earlier in this book is passed and enforced, the apportionment of the House of Representatives will remain unchanged. Each state will still be guaranteed at least one representative so long as all the other districts created have as close to the same population as possible.

► **We should create a general federal election**. The President and Vice President should continue to be elected as a team. However, the president and vice president should be elected independently of Congress since they are national, even if they are on the same ballot. This would fall short of creating a full parliamentary system in the U.S., although citizens should vote for the executive branch at the same time as Congress.

The 22nd amendment that limits a President to two terms should, therefore, be abolished. Presidential elections should continue to be held every four years, along with Congressional elections. Democracy itself is a term-limit mechanism since voters can remove an official by voting them out. Therefore, preventing somebody from running as often as they wish does not make sense. By abolishing executive branch term limits, we would subject Presidential elections to the same waves of public opinions as the simultaneous Congressional elections, thereby creating general elections which reflect the same will of the voters on those winning all offices in a given federal election.

► **We should allow binding national referenda on policy issues**. By incorporating some direct democracy via referenda, citizens would be empowered to enact legislation in the face of Congressional inaction or partisan gridlock. If we require signatures from at least one percent of eligible voters in at least a majority of Congressional districts to get a measure on the ballot, we will create a sufficiently high bar to ensure that we will not be inundated with referenda.

Taken together, these constitutional changes should be sufficient to fundamentally alter the current path of the United States government and steer it in the direction of democracy while maintaining many of the familiar characteristics of the original constitution. The impact of these changes would be to tie the government much more closely to public opinion and the perceived needs of voters through the mechanisms of general elections.

An important corollary to these reforms would cause the system to be more responsive to majorities and less responsive to elites. This would have the effect of limiting the de facto special interest veto power that has evolved in the present system through the interaction of our separation of powers and campaign finance systems. Elite groups are currently able to leverage their power and gain what they want by exploiting the need for concurrent majorities. These groups hold the system hostage by withholding their consent to needed legislation and policy unless their demands are met.

While many representative democratic political systems have adopted a parliamentary structure rather than a separation of powers structure because that system has proven to more accurately reflect public opinion within the political system, this bundle of reforms stops short of that. Why stop short? The stout belief in the wisdom of a separation of powers system within the American political psyche makes it very unlikely that our political culture will allow us to truly embrace parliamentary democracy.

Instead of the majority party in the legislature picking the executive, as is customary in parliamentary systems, this American version of democracy would maintain some of the separation of powers structure adopted by the founders and so enshrined in our political culture via an independent judicial branch and an independently elected executive branch. This may not be a system as democratic as we can get in an ideal world, but it is likely the most democracy that is within our grasp, or close enough to our grasp to justify striving to reach it.

Chapter Twenty

Proportional Representation: Pros and Cons

Continuing our catalogue of incremental democratic reforms, we next consider proportional representation.

In most modern democracies, the entire body of enfranchised citizens remains sovereign in principle because it chooses those who govern. In practice, though, day-to-day political power is exercised by elected representatives and those they appoint within a representative democratic system.

As the Stanford Encyclopedia of Philosophy (Stanford University, 2011) observed, "The concept of political representation is misleadingly simple: everyone seems to know what it is, yet few can agree on any particular definition. In fact, there is an extensive literature that offers many different definitions of this elusive concept. Hanna Pitkin (1967) provides, perhaps, one of the most straightforward definitions: to represent is simply to 'make present again'. On this definition, political representation is the activity of making citizens' voices, opinions, and perspectives 'present' in the public policy making processes."

The classic distinction among ideas of good representation is between *delegates* who simply follow what constituents believe (as expressed in elections, polls, and similar measures) and *trustees* who follow their own understanding of what is best.

Political scientist Pitkin argues in her influential *The Concept of Representation.* (Univ. of California Press, 1967) that neither makes sense alone. She holds that citizens can safeguard both their right to be represented and the autonomy of their representatives through a system that requires representatives to uphold democracy in general and support constituents' objective and genuine interests simultaneously. In such a framework, representatives agree to be held accountable to constituents while they preserve considerable leeway to exercise independent judgment.

Aside from the difficulty of determining what constituents' objective interests are and resolving conflicts among public opinion, this framework favors weighting representative democracy toward the trustee theory of representation. In an era when public opinion can be measured accurately and often, the delegate theory is at least far more practical, if not morally preferable, than it was in 1789, and deserves some consideration. It can be argued, though, that it too is inherently unsatisfactory because the ultimate way to empower citizens is not through delegate representatives but directly through the self-government of direct or participatory democracy.

Democracy is not a spectator sport, it's a participatory event. If we don't participate in it, it ceases to be a democracy.

—Michael Moore

Proportional Representation as a Democratic Alternative

If we are going to stick with representative democracy made more directly democratic by direct referenda so as not to break too radically from the American political tradition, we should recognize that there is another contender for the best form of representation: proportional representation. Can it improve American democracy without creating as many problems as it solves? Conceivably so, but before we embrace it, some analysis and cautions are in order.

Proportional representation is an electoral system in which the number of seats in a governing body such as a legislature is determined by the proportion of votes received in an election. For example, if we had three political parties in a political system, a left, center and right party and, in a hypothetical election, the left party received 42% of the vote, the center party tallied 26% of the vote, and the right party got 32% of the vote for seats in a 435 member legislature, the left party would get 183 seats, the center party would get 113, and the right party would get 139. Since none received an absolute majority, a coalition would need to be negotiated to form the legislative leadership.

By contrast, if those were the results in a winner-take all (non-proportional) national election (such as for the Presidency) or in each individual Congressional district election, the party polling the highest number of votes would win *all* the seats unless there were a requirement for an absolute majority of more than 50 % for election. In the latter case, a runoff election between the two highest vote-getters would determine who got all the seats. The minority (actually, a 58 % collective majority in this example) would be disenfranchised.

In short, proportional representation (PR) reflects the proportion of the total support of the electorate a given group earns in an election as opposed to a majority-takes-all way of counting votes. It is makes a lot of sense as a democratic reform if we our goal is to seek the most transparent form of representative democracy, one that most directly translates public support and votes into government seats.

The simplest way to achieve PR is to have multiple-member voting districts, either by state or the entire nation so voters express their preferences for all seats either by the laborious but perfectly democratic process of casting individual ballots (435 in this case), or by casting all their votes for a political party.

In general, proportional representation has some advantages. The most important of these is its fairness and transparency. Because each important stripe of ideology and policy belief in the spectrum of public opinion is faithfully transmitted to the legislature, it represents more people in the system more than a winner-take-all arrangement that can effectively disenfranchise either a significant minority or even an actual majority more of public opinion, as per our previous example of a simple three-party system.

Another important advantage of a PR system is that it usually leads to the likelihood of a greater voter turnout than in a winner-take-all system because participation by majorities and minorities alike is rewarded with a share of power, thereby giving people an incentive to get involved.

Along the same lines, PR also encourages a functioning free marketplace of ideas and bringing minorities into the system because a group of like-minded people only needs to get a small minority of the vote to be represented. It allows them to set up a stall in the free marketplace of ideas and bid for a larger minority or even a majority status with the power of their ideas.

Another advantage of PR is the educative role that it would play. Caroline J. Tolbert and Daniel A. Smith suggest in the article in *Representation*, (Vol. 42, No. 1, 2006) that "…the educative effects of the process on civic engagement, political participation, interest groups and political parties may prove to be equally, or more, important than any policy resulting…" Though the process they were referring to was direct democracy rather than proportional representation, their point applies to PR as well because of its encouragement of political participation and strengthening of political parties as aggregators and articulators of public opinion.

But despite its appeal, proportional representation is not a representational panacea. It can be fraught with significant problems. We need to approach this reform with caution in a pluralistic society such as the United States because of its potential side effects and unintended consequences.

One problem is its complexity. In order for a given election or electoral system to be truly proportional, each voter has to decide on the entire list. In a presidential election, that would not be a major issue and could even be an advantage because PR could serve to take the place of primary elections. In the case of a general U.S. House of Representatives election, though, voters ideally would need to be familiar with each candidate for all 435 seats unless they voted for all the candidates of a given political party. Such complexity would require a lot of voter time and research and media coverage. It assumes a level of voter effort, and familiarity with the issues and personalities, that substantially exceeds the current voter behavior of the vast majority of citizens in the United States.

Another problem of PR is its tendency toward electoral fragmentation. If each segment of public opinion (and perhaps social, economic, religious and geographic affinities, to name but a few of the possible components of a like-minded group) were transparently and faithfully represented in the political system, there might be so many parties and factions that none could get an effective governing majority. The proliferation of fragmentary groups that would be encouraged by this could even lead to political instability and become a threat to the viability of the entire political system if it proceeds too far. This is especially dangerous in a pluralistic and diverse political system that has serious economic, social, religious and ideological stratification.

The society and political system of the United States has so far been able to assimilate diversity and fragmentation over time (with the glaring exception of the War Between The States) by the leavening effect of a two-party system encouraged by a winner-take-all electoral system. It is unclear if a proportional representation system of representative democracy, if adopted, could contain the diversity of contemporary American politics and society over time.

While this could be a problem, it is containable. An effective way to make dangerous fragmentation less likely is to require a threshold percentage of the vote for a political party to be eligible for a continuous place on the ballot. In most PR systems, while any party or group can run once, any group that does not poll at least five percent (or whatever single-figure number is mandated) is not eligible to run again. This compromise is an attempt to strike a balance between proportional representation and political stability and makes sense to me.

Integrating PR Into the Existing System

In his book *Building a Democratic Political Order: Reshaping American Liberalism in the 1930s and 1940s,* (Cambridge University Press, 1996) David Plotke argues that representation has a central positive role in democratic politics: He suggests that we should try to improve representative practices and forms to make them more open, effective, and fair. Adopting at least some forms of proportional representation could accomplish these goals without totally changing the American political system.

One way to accomplish this, albeit slightly less democratic than the scheme we discussed earlier, would be to have state-based PR for U.S. House elections and national PR for U.S. Senate elections. Under this slightly less sweeping electoral reform, U.S. House of Representative elections could be by state, with each voter having, in effect, the number of votes equal to his or her state's number of House representatives. Voters would be able to distribute their ballots among the individual candidates or cast one vote collectively for all the state's U.S. Representative candidates of one party.

Under this proposal, the expanded Senate of 200 members mentioned earlier would be subject to national PR, with each contending party fielding a slate of 200 candidates in a national election. Again, voters would be able to distribute their 200 votes among the 200 candidates, or cast one vote collectively for all the Senatorial candidates of one party.

If the entire Congress (House of Representatives and Senate) were elected simultaneously, the result would move us closer to a general election than the present system provided that Presidential elections were also included on the same ballot.

Presidential candidates, as previously discussed, could either be elected from a national list and use a runoff system in a later election if no candidate received a majority, or we could use regional primaries or a national primary to screen the oversupply of candidates so only two or three would contend in the general election.

This hybrid system would go a long way toward reconciling the founders' desire to maintain an independent executive and a Senate that answers to a different (national) constituency than the House of Representatives with my desire to introduce more democracy into the political system.

Chapter Twenty One

How To Democratize the American Political System

In their 2014 book *The Fourth Revolution, The Global Race to Reinvent the State*, John Micklethwait and Adrian Wooldridge make a compelling case that democracy has been the driver for many of the laudable social achievements of the nation state in modern history. They also show that more democracy in today's nation-states will lead to more economic opportunity, social mobility, and freedom for their populations.

They write, "Democracy remains a huge advantage for the West. For all its messiness, it forces the state to respond to people's worries as well as allowing it to tap their talents. But democracy also needs to be reformed if it is to work properly; prevented from indulging its worst instincts and encouraged to express its best. The case for …extending liberty…is also a case for restoring democracy to its full potential."

They are largely correct. Democracy has many advantages as a reliable and effective way of governing modern nation-states. It allows them to provide benefits and opportunities for citizens while simultaneously limiting the costly excesses of runaway state collectivism and dictatorships. It is also the most self-correcting of all political systems because, through general elections, citizens can and do change entire governments and thereby change the entire direction of public policies.

Throughout this book, I have been advancing the case for democracy in 21st century America. But just making a case does not make change. The important question to ask is how do we steer this giant ship of state in a more democratic direction?

When considering answers to this question, my bias is to adopt strategies and tactics that maintain as much of our political tradition as possible to make change easier. This will lessen the chances of unleashing revolutionary violence that not only wreaks destruction but also fails to accomplish the goals sought.

Our challenge is to build agreement among thought leaders that the United States is not as democratic as it can be. We need to get those who are in a position to make policy to understand and endorse the idea that a truer democracy would be beneficial for our political system. Such agreement is certainly not present with a majority of opinion makers in the nation. By itself, that would not be an insurmountable problem over the long haul as long as we can build enough critical mass to gain media traction and sustain a national debate. Ultimately, the goal is to grow it into a sustained movement that can influence public opinion and create democratic constitutional change.

> *I have absolutely no idea what my generation did to enrich our democracy. We dropped the ball. We entered a period of complacency and closed our eyes to the public corruption of our democracy.*

> —Wynton Marsalis

What Needs To Be Done To Move Toward Democracy

Those who advocate democracy in the United States need to create enough noise and draw enough attention to the cause to create the momentum that will change the tone of our national political discourse into a democratic conversation. It can be done. As Doris Kearns Goodman points out in *The Bully Pulpit: Theodore Roosevelt, William Howard Taft and the Golden Age of Journalism* (Simon and Schuster, 2013), there have been several times in U.S. history when we crossed a political and cultural Rubicon and emerged transformed on the other side. The Civil War, the regulatory changes brought about by muckrakers and Progressives in the early 20th century, and the depression-era creation of a social safety net were such transformations. Our goal is to add a democratic transformation to the list.

► **Capturing Our Institutions.** We need to convince our political parties and political commentators that the gridlock malaise facing our political system and the disconnect between Americans and their government is real and dysfunctional. This unhealthy situation must be addressed.

Micklethwait and Wooldridge are right when saying that the American political right needs to give up its addiction to crony capitalism while the political left needs to give up its reflexive support for relentless state growth because both fuel an ideological addiction to a reflexive opposition within government. Both need to realize that the state has an important but not unlimited role to play. Micklethwait and Wooldridge say, "It [government] really matters, but it needs to be reinvented." They are correct on both counts. Moreover, any reinvention of government needs to involve more democracy to keep it on track and to prevent despotism.

The emergence of a robust democratic coalition and the conversion of our major political institutions into democratic agents of change will not just happen. This transition will require strong, articulate and persistent leaders in academia, journalism and government who champion the democratic cause. Given the current fragmentation of the media, it also needs to span multiple platforms to capture and hold the high ground of public opinion.

▶ **Sticking Within Our Political Culture.** A peaceful, effective movement for democratic change in the U.S. must be firmly rooted in the American political culture because failure to do so would severely limit its prospects for success and put it in a position to be falsely labeled as "Un-American" and thereby marginalized. It will require nothing less than a national recognition of the problems we face as a nation. It will also require a national willingness to deal with our problems both institutionally and ideologically. We need to steer a consistent course toward democracy and to carefully plan the way to get there and who we want to be onboard when we arrive.

Institutionally, we have inherited a deliberately-inefficient separation of powers system established by the founders because they distrusted public opinion. They had doubts about allowing those without property to participate. The latter has changed but the former has not. So we must work within that system even if it means stopping short of an optimal parliamentary system with general elections.

▶ **Using the System To Change It.** An interesting effort toward the kind of peaceful change I advocate is the Mayday Political Action Committee (MPAC) started by Harvard Law School Professor Larry Lessig. Calling itself a "crowd-funded Super PAC to end all Super PACs," MPAC raised $5 million as of this writing from 48,500 donors. This Super PAC is an independent political action committee that aims to elect a Congress committed to campaign finance reform. In 2014, The Mayday Political Action Committee will pilot this idea by running independent campaigns in 5 districts across the country. If successful, MPAC is planning to launch a

135

much larger campaign in 2016 with the goal of electing a majority of Congress that has either co-sponsored, or pledged to support, fundamental election finance reform in the way elections are funded.

This PAC further plans to press the Congress in 2017 to pass and the President to sign legislation that fundamentally reforms election funding and, ultimately, to achieve some version of publically-funded elections.

On MPAC's radar also, is to enact a constitutional amendment that would prohibit the ability of either wealthy individuals or groups like corporations or unions to spend unlimited amounts on political elections and to contribute unlimited amounts to independent political action committees. There are other groups working toward this end as well.

► **Working Within the Framework of American Political Culture to Develop a Unified Coalition.** Ideologically, Americans have a deep-seated belief that a separation of powers system is the best way to govern. Evidence to the contrary is not usually even offered, much less considered in most of our civic debate. So we are forced to work within that powerful cultural mindset. However, we should make a deliberate effort to raise public awareness of possible alternative scenarios and their advantages. We need to make democracy an important part of our civic debate and mindset.

Another important facet of our political culture is a strong belief in liberty and its historical companion, a near-fanatical support of limited government in principle, if not in practice. Americans have stubbornly maintained this belief even as the national, state and local governments grew steadily in scope and complexity as we dealt with legitimate policy needs throughout our history.

In other words, our political culture has two seemingly irreconcilable streams of influence flowing within it. These are actually differing responses to the same issues and different prescriptions for fixing what ails us. Somehow, we need to reconcile these differences in a coalition that recognizes the value of both liberty and the state as a medium of securing that liberty along with equality. Pro-liberty and pro-state advocates can and should unite on democracy as a way to secure their aims without negating the aspirations of the other.

Libertarians, for example, argue that severe limitations to the power and size of the nation-state and more liberty to pursue individual economic interests lead to a better society. They feel that a bare minimum of regulation and laws to keep the peace allows the talented to accumulate wealth and create free-enterprise institutions that redistribute enough wealth throughout the social and economic system to make life good for all people with initiative.

The other stream, the liberal statists, are liberal precisely because they strongly support the value of liberty that has characterized Western liberalism for more than four centuries. They are also statists because they support a fairly large role for the state in modern society because of its historic achievements in providing opportunity for the many and in balancing liberty and equality. Liberals also recognize that good states can avoid the excesses of collectivism and unbridled liberty through democracy. They have a concomitant belief that excessive economic liberty leads to an unbalanced concentration of wealth, economic exploitation and a society of a few haves versus the many have-nots. .

Without trying to resolve their differences, it is sufficient in this context to recognize that their common participation in American political culture and experience stands them together on a fairly large common ground. They both believe in variations on the theme that an appropriately-sized state limited and steered by democracy can accomplish the common good.

While libertarians emphasize a part of what a good democratic society needs: a large amount of liberty which provides a people the freedom to pursue their goals and ideals. They tend to downplay the possibility that each individual while pursuing his or her liberty can lead to conflict and the denial of liberty for others. Further, although they do gloss over the excesses of the robber-barons and unbridled economic liberty, they do support American democracy in principle.

The liberal statists, on the other hand, zealously emphasize the beneficial role of government in regulating a needed to balance liberty and equality in a good democratic society. Contemporary liberals tend to downplay the importance of liberty in practice despite their adherence to it in principle. They emphasize the equality-producing capabilities of the state. This ideology, for example, causes liberals to want to limit the allowable governmental surveillance of the American people and the ability to continually engage in war. These ideals put liberals in the same democratic camp with the libertarians.

Neither liberals nor libertarians have irreconcilable differences in bedrock political values. Both groups support liberty and equality, albeit with different degrees of emphasis. Both factions are willing to work with the system to pursue their aims. This commonality of ideals presents a solid basis of a platform for a coalition of democratic change in the United States. By emphasizing the ideals they hold in common and by demonstrating a willingness to compromise on the issues of liberty versus equality, the more thoughtful elements among each camp can unite. By so doing, these united factions can create, a movement that supports democracy as the best road to acceptable amounts of both liberty and equality.

▶ **Tactical Choices.** Should such a coalition become a third party or should it maintain itself as a nonpartisan movement? Frankly, it matters little. Because of institutionalized single-member districts that favor two parties over multiple parties, third parties have traditionally had their ideas co-opted by one or both major parties in order to steal their electoral thunder. Third parties have succeeded by having their policies adopted by the mainstream parties and the elites that support them.

Once such a coalition emerges, it has to decide the best tactics for constitutional change since to cross the Rubicon of American democracy will require substantial constitutional change. The real question is, "Should the movement advocate a constitutional convention or should it pursue constitutional change though amendments enacted by Congress and ratified by the states?" To me, this is an easy choice. Congressionally-initiated action that is driven by public opinion is preferable. Such congressional action would prevent the free-for-all that a constitutional convention is almost sure to devolve. It would limit the ability of powerful special interests to hijack the agenda in an era of Citizens United vs. The Federal Elections Commission and the ability of special interest money to dominate the airwaves.

Towards a New American Civic Ethic: Increasing Fairness and Opportunity

In the preceding chapter, we sketched what a democratically-invigorated constitution might look like. The question remains what else needs to be done within American political system and its underlying political culture to make the nation more receptive to democracy. Beyond the institutional changes, we need to strive to make the political system of the nation fairer and increase the opportunity for each person to participate meaningfully.

▶ **First, we need to reestablish the legitimacy of government.** Instead of denigrating government and oppo sing taxes and government spending in principle, we should recognize that democratic government can be a force for good. Through applying efficiency measures relentlessly to government we can assure that we get our money's worth for our tax dollars. Like insurance, if we put resources and risks into a common pool, we have the ability to deal with problems in a timely and cost-effectively manner.

▶ **Next we need to make politics honorable again.** Along with a renewed appreciation of democratic government should come a recognition that government service is honorable and deserves as much respect in peacetime as in wartime. A universal Civic Action Corps, fashioned in the order of the Peace Corps or the depression-era Civilian Conservation Corps, should be created. This corps could be used to repair our crumbling infrastructure, to defend our nation, to shore up our educational system, to assimilate immigrants, and to respond to a broad cross section of social needs. We can add fairness to the equation if, going forward, we require a couple of years of public service in a suitable field for all citizens at age 18. We should reward those who serve with a fair wage while they serve and the right to a subsidized education (academic or vocational, as appropriate) upon completion of their service.

We end as we began: by recognizing that American exceptionalism is more of a myth than a reality today because we are not world leaders in education, equality, and a host of other desirable things. But we recognize

139

that it does not have to be that way. The United States of America can regain its pre-eminence in a lot of important international arenas. Through a renewed commitment to live up to our potential and a vigorous embracement of democracy, we can become who we already believe we are.

America needs nothing less than relentless self-education on what democracy is and what it can accomplish for us. We need a commitment by citizens and leaders alike to press forward on this for as long as it takes to get the job done. I believe American is up to it—but we need to begin.

About The Author

Jeffrey R. Orenstein earned his B.A. from Ohio State University in Columbus, Ohio and an M.A. and Ph.D. from the University of Wisconsin-Madison, all in political science.

His first career was in education, starting as an Assistant Professor of Political Science at Kent State University in Ohio in the 1970's and taking an early retirement as a full professor 25 years later.

He is the co-author of several books in the field, including *An Introduction to Political Theory* (New York: HarperCollins, 1993), co-authored with Robert Booth Fowler, the University of Wisconsin-Madison, *U. S. Rail Policy: Uncle Sam at the Throttle* (Chicago: Nelson-Hall, 1990), *Contemporary Issues in Political Theory, Revised Edition* (New York: Greenwood, 1985). Co-authored with Robert Booth Fowler, the University of Wisconsin-Madison and *Contemporary Issues in Political Theory* (New York: John Wiley and Sons, 1977).

His current career is in journalism. He is the Publisher and Executive Editor of *Living On The Suncoast Magazine*, entering its tenth year of publication and has been the executive editor of *The Gulf Coast Business Review*, both in Sarasota.

He has written numerous articles on transportation and technology issues for national magazines and his most recent book is *You Can Write A Book: How To Write What You Know and Self-Publish Your Way to Success*, (Sarasota, Suncoast Digital Press, 2013), co-authored with Barbara Bingham.

He and his wife Virginia live in Lakewood Ranch, Florida.

Connecting With The Author

If you agree that the United States Government is broken and needs to be fixed, please connect with me by liking our Facebook Page at www.facebook.com/FixingingAmericanGovernment and visiting www.FixingAmericanGovernment.com. Complete contact information is available there and updates and further information will be posted there too. I welcome your ideas and perspectives whether you agree with me or not.

If you found this book to be useful and informative, please consider writing a short review of it at Amazon.com or other book review site. For Amazon, scroll down to the Customer Reviews section and click on the tab marked "Write A Customer Review."

I appreciate your feedback and will use it to improve future iterations of this book.

Thank you for your support.

Jeffrey R. Orenstein

Index

20th century 14, 25, 134
22nd 95, 110, 124
1789 70, 73, 81, 109, 121, 128

A

Adam Smith 21
administration 57, 64, 91, 93, 95, 96
Adrian Wooldridge 133
Affordable Care Act 31, 64, 75
Afghanistan 29, 30, 55, 56
Africa 55
African-Americans 43
Alexander Hamilton 15, 22
Alexis de Tocqueville 9
Al Franken 94
Al Gore 109, 117
Al Qaeda 60
amendment 77, 84, 95, 103, 107, 110,
    122, 124, 136
America iii, vi, vii, 4, 5, 9, 10, 11, 13, 19,
    21, 24, 25, 29, 30, 34, 37, 38, 40,
    57, 60, 63, 69, 70, 75, 79, 106, 109,
    111, 119, 122, 133, 140
American exceptionalism 29, 33, 35, 57,
    139
American government 13, 44, 82
American politics vi, vii, 10, 30, 44, 46,
    130
American Revolution 21, 37, 62
Americans For Prosperity 47
Amtrak 40, 65
Andrew Young 106
anti-government 41, 63
Arab oil cartel 62
Aristotle iv
Army-McCarthy hearings 57
Articles of Confederation 15, 37, 38
Article VI 24
Athens iv, 3, 24
Aung San Suu Kyi 67, 71
Austria 43

B

ballot 27, 39, 43, 78, 79, 100, 105, 112,
    121, 124, 131
ballot box 27, 39
bed sheet ballots 45
Belgium 13, 43, 65
Benghazi, Libya 57
Benjamin Franklin 14
bicameral legislature 22
Bill Moyers 1, 21, 84
Bill of Rights 24, 44
bipartisanship 90
Birmingham, Alabama 43
British 7, 14, 25, 26, 37, 51, 61, 71
budget 17, 31, 33, 40, 64, 75, 92
Burt Neuborne 50
Bush vs. Gore 103

C

cable TV networks 70
California 27, 50, 51, 88, 127
campaign vi, 16, 26, 43, 46, 47, 53, 63,
    64, 79, 90, 93, 105, 107, 108, 111,
    112, 113, 116, 122, 123, 125, 135
campaign contributions 16, 107
campaign financing 122
Canada 27, 43, 65
candidate vi, 17, 23, 25, 47, 51, 94, 106,
    107, 109, 111, 112, 113, 114, 117,
    122, 130, 132
Candidates 88, 93, 105, 113
Caroline J. Tolbert 129
Caucus 17
caucuses 49, 114
Center for the Study of the American
    Dream 82
centralized power 25
Charles B. Rangel 77
checks and balances 14, 38
checks and balances system 26, 27
Chief Justice 103

China 13, 31, 34, 60
Chinese political thought 5
Chinua Achebe 44, 81
Christopher Skovron 87
Chrysler 64
circuit courts 99
citizen iii, 16, 45, 69, 79, 82, 83, 90, 105
citizens iii, iv, 1, 4, 11, 25, 26, 28, 31, 43,
44, 52, 59, 69, 70, 81, 82, 83, 105,
106, 109, 115, 116, 117, 119, 121,
124, 127, 128, 130, 133, 139, 140
Citizens 79, 81, 96, 103, 107, 108, 122,
139
civic 13, 26, 28, 31, 33, 43, 44, 45, 63, 69,
71, 74, 75, 76, 77, 81, 82, 83, 84,
85, 129, 136
civic education 44, 82, 83, 84, 85
Civics 13, 82
civil liberties 11, 25, 96, 103
Clare Boothe Luce 89
CNN 30, 34
coalition government 27
coalitions 52, 58
cold war 34, 57, 58
communications iv, 6, 70
competitiveness 40, 116
concurrent majority 16
Confucianism 5
Congress iii, 16, 17, 24, 26, 33, 49, 51,
56, 63, 64, 75, 77, 78, 87, 89, 90,
91, 94, 97, 101, 102, 106, 108, 110,
123, 124, 131, 135, 138
Congressional elections 43, 107, 115,
124
conservative 23, 25, 63, 87, 88
constitution 4, 9, 14, 23, 26, 38, 39, 69,
71, 72, 73, 77, 90, 93, 99, 100, 110,
117, 119, 120, 121, 122, 124, 139
Constitution C, 21, 23, 24, 25, 37, 50, 51,
69, 89, 119, 121
constitutional change 73, 76, 89, 90, 101,
120, 134, 138
constitutional convention 37, 120, 138
Constitutional Convention 14, 15, 21,
37, 38, 102

courts of original jurisdiction 99
crisis. iii
cultural norms 5

D

Daniel A. Smith 129
David Broockman 87
Declaration of Independence 14, 26
Deigo Von Vacaano 5
delegates 15, 22, 38, 102, 127
democracy iii, iv, v, vi, 1, 3, 4, 5, 6, 9, 10,
11, 13, 14, 15, 21, 22, 23, 24, 25,
26, 27, 28, 29, 30, 35, 38, 39, 41,
44, 45, 51, 52, 56, 59, 62, 67, 69,
71, 72, 75, 76, 77, 78, 81, 82, 83,
84, 85, 94, 95, 96, 103, 105, 106,
109, 111, 114, 116, 117, 119, 120,
121, 123, 124, 125, 127, 128, 129,
130, 132, 133, 134, 135, 136, 137,
138, 139, 140
Democracy In America 9, 10
democratic coalition 135
Democrats 16, 50, 77, 103
demographers 78
direct democracy iv, 3, 14, 24, 25
District Courts 91
divided government 26, 27
Dixiecrat 88

E

Edmund Burke 52
Edmund Randolph 15, 22
education 6, 28, 30, 31, 35, 38, 43, 44, 70,
81, 82, 84, 85, 139, 140, 141
Elbridge Gerry 15, 22
electing judges 101
elections 6, 7, 14, 22, 26, 27, 30, 41, 43,
45, 46, 47, 50, 77, 78, 81, 87, 88,
89, 90, 95, 96, 101, 105, 106, 107,
109, 110, 111, 112, 113, 114, 115,
116, 117, 121, 122, 123, 124, 127,
130, 131, 136

Elections 52, 77, 103, 105, 106, 107, 110, 111, 114, 116, 117, 139
electoral college 23, 26, 109
Electoral College 25, 26, 109, 117, 121
electoral system 102, 110, 111, 128, 130
enfranchisement v, 3, 16, 25, 121
English Reform Act of 1832 7
EOP 92, 93
equality iv, 5, 9, 10, 45, 69, 83, 136, 137, 138, 139
Eric Cantor 17, 51
Estonia 45
ethnic diversity 70
Europe 4, 5, 7, 24, 27, 31, 33, 56, 58, 62, 64, 72, 79
executive 7, 14, 22, 23, 27, 56, 91, 92, 93, 94, 95, 96, 97, 102, 124, 125, 132, 141
executive branch 56, 91, 92, 93, 94, 95, 97, 102, 124, 125
Executive Office of the Presidency 96
executives 16
Extraordinary majorities 123

F

faction 17, 22
FEC 108
federal district judges 99
Federal Election Commission 78, 79
Federalist No. 10 22
federal judicial branch 99, 100
federal system 40
filibuster 50, 88, 89, 90
Finley Peter Dunne 104
Florida vi, 16, 27, 43, 44, 45, 77, 141
foreign policy 28, 33, 55, 56, 57, 58, 59, 60, 74
franchise 14, 72
Francis Bellamy 13
Franklin D. Roosevelt 39, 92
freedom 4, 5, 11, 24, 29, 30, 31, 55, 59, 71, 85, 105, 116, 122, 133, 137
freedom of speech, press and assembly 5, 11

Free Marketplace of ideas 107

G

Gallup iii, 87
gay marriage 112
general election 7, 9, 13, 14, 26, 27, 46, 72, 73, 90, 93, 110, 119, 121, 122, 123, 124, 131, 132, 133, 135
general electorate 46, 96
General Motors 64
geographers 78
George Washington 22
George W. Bush 25, 63, 89, 109, 117
Germany 43, 65
gerrymandering 15, 16, 45, 51, 63, 77, 90, 109, 110, 116, 124
governing iii, 63, 94, 97, 122, 128, 130, 133
government iii, iv, v, 3, 4, 6, 7, 9, 10, 13, 14, 15, 16, 17, 21, 22, 23, 24, 26, 27, 28, 32, 34, 35, 37, 38, 39, 40, 41, 42, 43, 46, 49, 50, 55, 61, 62, 63, 64, 65, 69, 70, 71, 72, 73, 74, 75, 79, 81, 82, 83, 85, 89, 91, 92, 93, 96, 97, 99, 100, 102, 105, 106, 107, 108, 110, 112, 115, 119, 120, 121, 124, 129, 134, 135, 136, 137, 139
great depression 61, 102
Great Depression 61
Great Recession 64
Greek iv, 3
gridlock 26, 27, 46, 49, 50, 51, 52, 53, 57, 74, 75, 89, 124, 134
GRIO (NBC News) 43
ground game 43, 113

H

Hanna Pitkin 127
health care 33, 34, 64, 65
health front 31
House of Commons v, 43
House of Lords 51
Howard Zinn 29

145

I

ideological voters 46
incremental reforms 119
independent federal judiciary 122
Independents 103
indirect forms of representation. 23
infrastructure 6, 31, 33, 34, 38, 49, 59,
    62, 65, 72, 74, 82, 139
Interest groups 47
international system 34, 58, 71
interstate commerce clause 73
invisible hand 61, 65
Iraq 29, 30, 55, 58
Israel, 43

J

James Madison 15, 22, 102
Japan 13, 31
Jean Jacques Rousseau, iv
Jeb Bush 113
Jeremy Bentham iv
John F. Kennedy 58
John Locke iv
John Maynard Keynes 61
John Micklethwait 133
John Q. Adams 109
John Quincy Adams 25
John Stuart Mill iv, 4
John Winthrop 29
Joseph Biden 91
judicial independence 101, 103
judicial review 100, 102, 123

K

Kathryn Tuggle 63
Kennedy, John F. iii
Keynesian economic theory 62
Kofi Annan 30
Kyoto Treaty 35

L

laissez-faire 64, 71
lame duck 93, 95, 110

lame duck presidents 93
Larry Lessig 135
Larry Sabato 100
legislation 16, 17, 26, 44, 49, 50, 51, 52,
    59, 63, 64, 87, 88, 95, 96, 97, 102,
    106, 122, 123, 124, 125, 136
legislators 7, 14, 16, 23, 53, 56, 78, 87, 88
legislature 7, 14, 16, 73, 77, 90, 102, 116,
    122, 125, 128, 129
Level Playing Field 107
liberal democrat v
liberalism v, 137
liberal statists 137
libertarians 39, 62, 64, 137, 138
Libertarians 63, 137
liberty v, 5, 9, 15, 29, 45, 83, 120, 133,
    136, 137, 138
lifetime terms 100, 101
literacy 70, 81, 82, 83, 84, 109
Locke 7
low voter turnout 42, 43, 45, 74, 115

M

magistrates 4, 99, 101, 102
majority 4, 5, 7, 10, 14, 15, 16, 17, 22,
    23, 26, 27, 38, 44, 45, 49, 50, 62,
    63, 77, 78, 88, 89, 90, 93, 94, 100,
    101, 103, 109, 114, 115, 116, 119,
    123, 124, 125, 128, 129, 130, 132,
    134, 136
malapportionment 51
Marbury vs. Madison 102
marijuana legalization 112
Marshall Plan 56
Mayday Political Action Committee
    (MPAC) 135
media vii, 16, 41, 47, 49, 52, 70, 79, 85,
    89, 93, 99, 105, 108, 113, 115, 116,
    130, 134, 135
median household income 64
Mexico 45
Michael Moore 128
Michael Parenti 21
middle class 62, 63, 64, 65, 72

Middle East 29, 55, 58
mid-term Congressional elections 44
military aid 56
Milton Friedman 62
minority 5, 10, 14, 15, 17, 23, 25, 50, 51, 56, 62, 88, 90, 123, 128, 129
money in politics 79, 107, 122

N

National Public Radio 85
national referenda 78, 124
National Rifle Association 51
national security 96, 107
nation-state iv, 6, 137
negative ads 107, 116
Negative campaigning 46
New Deal 61, 92, 102
New England-style town meeting 13
Newsweek 44
New York 4, 37, 43, 56, 57, 141
Niels Bohr 96
Norman Ornstein 89
North Korea 5, 13
nuclear option 50, 51, 88, 90

O

oligarchies v, 73
one-person-one-vote standard 78
Open Access 106
overridden 16

P

Pandora's Box 120
paralysis 49
parliamentary 7, 14, 26, 27, 73, 89, 97, 124, 125, 135
partisan 49, 57, 75, 78, 83, 85, 87, 89, 103, 112, 113, 114, 124
partisanship 49, 52, 57, 94
party nominating conventions 114
passenger rail service 31
patriotism iii, 56, 69
patronage 91

pay to play 79
Pennsylvania 21, 38
petition 24, 112
Plato iv
Plum Book 91
political iii, iv, vi, vii, 3, 4, 5, 6, 7, 9, 10, 11, 13, 16, 17, 21, 22, 23, 24, 25, 26, 27, 28, 29, 31, 32, 33, 34, 35, 37, 41, 43, 44, 45, 46, 47, 49, 52, 55, 56, 57, 58, 61, 64, 69, 70, 71, 72, 73, 75, 76, 77, 78, 79, 81, 82, 83, 84, 85, 87, 89, 91, 94, 95, 97, 100, 102, 103, 104, 105, 106, 107, 108, 110, 111, 112, 113, 115, 119, 120, 121, 122, 125, 127, 128, 129, 130, 131, 132, 133, 134, 135, 136, 137, 138, 139, 141
political culture vii, 10, 21, 25, 29, 35, 37, 43, 71, 72, 73, 77, 112, 115, 119, 125, 135, 136, 137, 139
political parties 27, 41, 43, 47, 52, 78, 95, 105, 128, 129, 134
Political scientist 10, 21, 127
political scientists 13, 25, 37, 72, 78, 83, 84
political system iii
poll 44, 87, 109, 131
PR 129, 130, 131
president 23, 44, 89, 91, 92, 94, 95, 96, 97, 100, 101, 110, 124
Presidential appointments 50, 87, 89
Presidential nomination 16
Presidential primary 114
presidential transition 93, 96
primaries 46, 93, 94, 95, 114, 132
primary 17, 31, 41, 46, 51, 88, 93, 94, 95, 113, 114, 130, 132
Progressive movement 25, 41
property-owning White males 21
property qualifications for voters 27
proportional representation 127, 128, 129, 130, 131
proximate 75, 76, 77, 81, 97, 106
public financing of campaigns 79, 96, 108, 122

public office vi, vii, 23, 52, 111, 112, 113, 116
public officials vii, 44
public opinion iv, v, vi, 7, 13, 14, 16, 27, 33, 41, 46, 47, 51, 64, 87, 90, 93, 95, 106, 113, 114, 119, 121, 124, 125, 127, 129, 130, 134, 135, 138
public policy v, vii, 44, 70, 79, 93, 102, 107, 127
public radio 85
public service 42, 139
public television 85

R

referendum 14, 27, 111, 112
reform 33, 69, 73, 75, 76, 95, 96, 102, 103, 108, 129, 130, 131, 135
registered voters 43, 112
regulation of the economy 41
representation 23, 27, 51, 88, 90, 123, 127, 128, 131
representative iv, 6, 7, 10, 13, 25, 27, 72, 76, 121, 122, 123, 124, 125, 127, 128, 129, 130, 131
representative democracy 6, 7, 13, 25, 27, 121
republic 13, 14, 15, 21, 27, 73, 121
Republican 15, 17, 25, 63, 77, 87, 89, 110
Republicans 16, 45, 77, 88, 90, 103
Richard Cheney 91
Richard Price 81
Rick Scott 45
right wing 63, 89
Robert Booth Fowler vii, 4, 141
Robert Graham 44
Ronald Reagan 29, 63
Russia 13
Rutherford Hayes 109

S

Samuel Adams 15
Sarasota vi, 43, 141
self-government iv, 5, 24, 28, 128
Senate confirmation 22, 91, 100

Senate representation 50, 88
Senate rules 16, 88
Senatorial Courtesy 94
separation of powers system 17, 41, 49, 56, 76, 91, 99, 119, 125, 135, 136
Shay's Rebellion 120
Shays's Rebellion 22
ShelbyCounty vs. Holder 77
single party 45
Social Security 30, 61
social spending 65
Somalia, 58
Soviet Union 57
special courts 103
special interests 16, 41, 47, 90, 96, 107, 108, 120, 122, 139
spectrum 29, 46, 91, 108, 129
staggered elections 88
Stanford Encyclopedia of Philosophy 127
state courts 99
state legislatures 23, 26, 45, 63, 121
State of The Nation address 97
state primaries 95
states iv, 5, 6, 14, 16, 21, 23, 24, 25, 38, 49, 50, 52, 65, 70, 73, 77, 82, 83, 88, 94, 95, 100, 104, 109, 110, 115, 117, 120, 133, 137, 138
STEM 82
Super PAC 135
Supreme Court 16, 17, 26, 61, 73, 77, 79, 91, 94, 99, 100, 102, 103, 104, 107, 109, 117
Supreme Court Justices 17
Swiss cantons 24

T

Tea Party 17, 37, 39, 62, 63, 75, 88
technology iv, 31, 34, 47, 82, 111, 141
term limits 10, 24, 41, 53, 95, 101, 110, 124
terrorists 34, 60
The anti-war movement 57
Theodore C. Sorensen 6

Theodore Sorensen 92
The Patriot Act 59
The Public Broadcasting Service (PBS 85
Thomas Jefferson 19, 62, 81, 120
Thomas Mann 89
Thucydides iv, 3, 4
Todd Leopold 30
town-meeting iv
transportation 6, 31, 34, 38, 49, 59, 70, 141
Twitter 70
tyrants 120

U

unconstitional 77
undemocratic 23, 26, 100, 123
Union of Soviet Socialist Republics 34
United Kingdom 13
United States iii, vi, vii, 9, 10, 13, 15, 19, 21, 24, 25, 28, 29, 30, 32, 33, 34, 35, 37, 40, 43, 44, 49, 50, 55, 57, 60, 67, 69, 70, 71, 73, 75, 76, 77, 82, 83, 85, 91, 105, 106, 109, 111, 119, 124, 130, 133, 134, 138, 140, 141
United States Courts of Appeals 91
United States House of Representatives vi, 14, 16, 17, 25, 26, 27, 28, 63, 73, 90, 110, 121, 123, 124, 130, 131, 132
U.S. Chamber of Commerce 47
U.S. Constitution 9, 25, 102, 103, 110, 120, 121, 122
U.S. federal court system 100
U.S. Founders 14
U.S. House of Representatives 110

V

Venezuela 43
veto 14, 22, 26, 28, 50, 89, 123, 125
Vice President 91, 110, 124
Viet Nam 29, 30, 57
voter suppression laws 45, 109, 110
voter turnout 16, 43, 45, 52, 113, 114, 116, 129
Voting Rights Act 16, 77, 78, 84, 110, 115

W

Washington Post 5, 92
Western political thought 3
White House 26, 49, 92, 93, 97
White House Chief of Staff 92
William Harrison 109
William J. Clinton 50
William Stephens Smith 120
Winston Churchill v, 72
World War II 33, 34, 56, 57, 59, 62
Wynton Marsalis 134
Wyoming 27, 50, 51, 88

www.ingramcontent.com/pod-product-compliance
Lightning Source LLC
Chambersburg PA
CBHW060929040426
42445CB00011B/856